Connecting Your Journey with the Story of God:

Disciplemaking in Diverse Contexts
by Dave Livermore

For feedback, discussion or to learn more about Sonlife visit: www.sonlife.com

#S1311059

Contents

For feedback, discussion or to
learn more about Sonlife visit:
www.sonlife.com

I know of few things that bring me the joy and pain that my heart for the globe brings me. There are times I wish I could cut it out of my being. I wake up at night thinking about the billions of people who have yet to hear about Jesus. I find my mind suddenly wandering during a sharpening evening of interaction with friends, thinking about how to mobilize the wealth of resources in the West. My enjoyment of a holiday feast is interrupted by the thought of the millions of people starving, and the list goes on.

At the same time, seeing God's work around the world has allowed me to taste and experience God in unusual ways. I have seen him supersede in the midst of spiritual warfare. I have heard the testimonies of persecuted believers who know God in a much deeper way than I do. I have been challenged to question the assumptions my cultural lens brings my understanding of God and his Story.

It is with that paradoxical heart that I share the chapters that follow. I am in process as a child of the King and as a minister in his kingdom. This book begins with an overview of God's Story and its relevance to our respective ministries. Part I looks at our mission as believers and ministers in God's kingdom. We will consider the implications of Christ's mandate to make disciples and the unfolding of his plan, as well as look at the vehicles God has given us for carrying out his mandate. Part II digs into the process of ministry used by Jesus. This section begins by considering Christ's role prior to his earthly ministry, and then focuses on the way he went about his three years of earthly ministry with a glimpse into the growth of his ministry through the early church in the

Epistles. Part III asks you to consider the implications of God's Story for your own journey in ministry. Given your context, what does it mean to walk as Jesus walked? How does your life and ministry connect with the greater Story of God? These are questions with which I continue to wrestle as a minister committed to disciplemaking.

Thank you for the honor of traveling this journey with you.

Dave Livermore
International Director, Sonlife Ministries

CHAPTER ONE

Overview:
Engaging in the Story of God

I've only been in vocational ministry for about twelve years; but it didn't take me long to grow tired of formulaic, prescriptive answers to ministry. Believe me! The first few years in ministry I jumped at the chance to attend every seminar and read every book and article that promised me some measure of success.

A few ministries later, traveling to 30-some countries and perhaps more than anything else, being a parent—makes me more suspicious than ever of A+B=C approaches to ministry. There has been far more mystery to my ministry experiences than that!

At the same time, I cannot entirely accept the postmodern nihilism of many of my colleagues at the university where I'm completing graduate work. I can't accept that all we are to do is create our own story lines amid the randomness of life. Though life is full of mystery and tension, I'm confident God desires order; but my understanding of what that means is always thwarted. Yet I often feel like Hollywood's movies better engage the mind in thinking about spiritual matters than our three-point alliterated messages do. This should not be! Instead of giving up any sense of order or a ministry plan, I'm drawn to participating in a Story bigger than my ministry and me, and using that Story to construct a ministry plan that suits my unique context.

I am drawn to engagement with the Story of God. The Story of God is about God, by God, for God and through God. Christ is the means by which I connect with the Story of God and in so doing, my life and ministry are part of the Story! He is the whole point of the Story and he invites me to be part of it. Frank Buechner says it well:

> It is a world of magic and mystery, of deep darkness and flickering starlight. It is a world where terrible things happen and wonderful things too. It is a world where goodness is pitted against evil, love against hate, order against chaos, in a great struggle where often it is hard to be sure who belongs to which side because appearances are endlessly deceptive. Yet for all its confusion and wildness, it is a world where the battle goes ultimately to the good, who live happily ever after, and where in the long run everybody, good and evil alike, becomes known by his true name… That is the fairy tale of the gospel with, of course, one crucial difference from all other fairy tales, which is that the claim made for it is that it is true, that it not only happened once upon a time but has kept on happening ever since and is happening still.[1]

God was weaving his Story before the beginning of time and continues to weave it today in my heart and yours, and in my ministry and yours. The heroes are not really David, Moses, Paul, Augustine, Oswald Chambers or Mother Teresa. Jesus is the only true hero. Ultimately, the rest of us are all villains.

Christ is the first and the last. Even the Bible is not the point. It is a means to the end—Jesus! As I use the Word to get to know him and make him known to others, I am not lord over it, it is lord over me. I must be more concerned about using it to interpret me, my journey with God and my ministry with him than thinking I can come in and objectively interpret the text. The goal is not so much to remove all my biases, but rather to have an honest understanding of the biases I'm inclined to import into the text.

A growing number of excellent resources are available that exhort character development based on reconstructing our understanding of the Story of God. I am not suggesting we can separate the two. However,

I'm inclined to raise the same issue as it pertains to ministry. Without creating one more prescriptive ministry model, how can we reconstruct our understanding of Jesus and biblical history to re-encounter the Story of God and understand our ministries in light of it? What does the Story mean for my life in the kingdom and for my pursuit of leading others in the kingdom?

I don't intend to answer these questions exhaustively, but to stimulate some thinking in this regard. I will challenge assumptions and raise more questions regarding ministry in diverse cultural settings.

The resurgence of attention given in recent years to answering the question, "What would Jesus do?" as we go about our daily lives has been monumental. Unfortunately, as ministry leaders we often fail to ask the same question as it pertains to our own leadership. If Jesus were in my shoes, with my set of experiences, with my cultural context and in my church, how would he lead my ministry?

If Jesus were in my shoes, with my set of experiences, with my cultural context and in my church, how would he lead my ministry?

The answer lies in looking at the Story of God and its hero, Jesus. How did Jesus approach ministry 2,000 years ago in his context? He never held a public office, never wrote a book, never conducted workshops, never founded an organization. His classroom was the boat and the field, and his students were simple fishermen. Rejected and misunderstood by the majority, his ministry only lasted three and a half years. Yet its impact changed global history!

Jesus said, "As the Father has sent me, I am sending you" (John 20:21). His life serves as an example not just in the words he taught, but in the way he went about ministry. Howard Hendricks recognizes this when he asks, "How did Jesus Christ train his men? Whenever we study the Gospels, we tend to study them exclusively for content. Why don't we study them for methodology?"[2]

The pages which follow are an opportunity to do just that—to take an intensive look at the life and ministry of Jesus as the basis for constructing our respective ministry strategies. The term "strategy" is not meant to imply methods or a particular model of ministry. I am confident Jesus would use very different methods if he came into Asia in the 21st century. However, I expect the overall process and philosophy guiding those methods would be the same as what he used 2,000 years ago, and what we have seen as characteristic of him all throughout the ages. Obviously there were unique aspects to Jesus' approach given his context, just as Joseph, Jeremiah and Paul had unique approaches. However, what transcended their unique contexts? What elements of the Story continually surface and mandate our attention for ministry today? While keeping the full scope of the narrative in mind, I will focus primarily on Christ's earthly model as the laboratory.

To what degree should we read the Gospels as *prescriptive* for ministry today and to what degree are they mainly *descriptive* of Christ's approach to ministry in his context? I am uncomfortable with either extreme. I am not interested in simply preserving or restoring biblical approaches to disciplemaking. We cannot fulfill the will of God in some anachronistic manner by resurrecting prophetic bands, disciple groups or apostolic teams. However, we can and must discover contextually appropriate approaches to making disciples that resonate in fundamental ways with the organic process modeled best by Christ.[3]

> However, we can and must discover contextually appropriate approaches to making disciples that resonate in fundamental ways with the organic process modeled best by Christ.

The calling of God on my life is to train, coach and mentor local church disciplemakers for every people group of the world. Therefore, understanding the use of Christ's process of ministry in diverse contexts is of utmost importance to me. As I get a better grasp of the whole Story of God, I find Christ's process of ministry transcending the unique context and time period in which he ministered.

Sonlife, the ministry in which I am privileged to serve, gives me the platform and resources to live out my calling. Allow me to share a little about our vision for the globe so you understand the context from which I write the pages that follow.

Sonlife's corporate mission is to restore to the heart of the local church a passion for Great Commission and Great Commandment living. We want to see the church be the church, multiplying itself personally and corporately. We believe God has called us to mobilize 100,000 churches in North America over the next ten years to multiply personally and corporately. Personally, we are challenging, motivating and equipping pastors to shepherd multiplying ministries wherein each year for every hundred people in the ministry, ten people embrace Christ as Lord and are assimilated into the local church. Corporately, we are challenging churches to multiply by planting another church locally or cross-culturally every three years.

Internationally, our vision is the same. We want to see the church be the church by multiplying itself all over the world. We want to work with proven multipliers in every people group of the world. We are committed to mobilizing younger leaders as a key strategy for fulfilling this vision.

In short, we envision passionate leaders on six continents training, coaching and mentoring others for personal and corporate multiplication. Specifically, we envision:

- A proven multiplier in each major region of the world who embraces the vision to passionately strategize, reaching that nation through younger leaders
- A proven leader in each country of the world with a vision to mobilize the church throughout that country through younger leaders
- Great Commission, healthy churches penetrating every people group in every country through personal and corporate multiplication

Sonlife has four values that run through our ministries around the world as common threads:

1. Christ's Strategy Contextualized

We are committed to coming alongside national churches to implement Christ's model of disciplemaking in a culturally relevant manner. Both Christ's strategy and contextualization are important to us. You will see that in the way this book is presented, first looking at Jesus' process of ministry and then considering its implications for unique contexts.

Christ's Strategy Contextualized:

We are committed to coming alongside national churches to implement Christ's model of disciplemaking in a culturally relevant manner.

We are committed to Christ's strategy of ministry. Churches everywhere can learn something from the organic process of ministry modeled by Jesus and further demonstrated by the early church. We are convinced this is the way to make disciples of all nations.

At the same time, we are highly committed to contextualization. Even though our materials have traditionally been philosophy-oriented rather than program-oriented, we have never been interested in simply translating our materials into every language possible. We understand that contextualization is far more complex than that. Furthermore, we believe long-term, indigenous church leaders are the best multipliers of the disciplemaking process contextually, though cross-cultural missionaries continue to be needed to equip these leaders and to move into frontier fields.

This is more than just theory to me. One of the greatest privileges of my ministry is getting to see first hand the implementation of Christ's process of ministry in diverse contexts around the world. It looks radically different in many places, yet consistently, the process of multiplication remains sound and true everywhere.

2. Younger Leaders Mobilized

Younger Leaders Mobilized:

We are committed to mobilizing younger leaders to fuel a movement of multiplication.

We are committed to mobilizing younger leaders to fuel a movement of multiplication. Our focus on younger leaders is driven by the proven return of investing in youth. God uniquely used youth throughout Israel's history and many of Jesus' disciples were younger leaders—some may well have been under twenty. Throughout church history, God has continued to use younger leaders to expand the kingdom. Some of the most aggressive church planting movements in the world today are being led by younger leaders.

In many places around the world, mobilizing younger leaders may happen through segmented ministry to youth, but not in all places. Sonlife is less interested in exporting Westernized youth ministry and more interested in waving the flag for investing in youth as leaders in the church. We understand that in many parts of the world, youth alone cannot turn around a nation or a church. Many Eastern cultures respect the elderly first and foremost. Regardless, even in these contexts, we believe God will use younger leaders to fuel a movement of multiplication that is global in scope.

For example, Pastor Abraham Sahu, one of our key partners in India, is developing a school of evangelism for younger leaders. He is purposely investing in young men ages 18-30 to prepare them as church planters and pastors in India and beyond. The training process is a minimum of two years. The first year the younger leaders are trained for two months, they implement the training in local ministries for the next four months and then repeat that cycle the second half of the year. The second year, the first two months are again devoted to training. The younger leaders go into the various ministry sites for the next eight months and then come back for the final two months of the two-year process for debriefing and final release. Abraham is working in a culture in which elders are given utmost respect and he is committed to not circumventing the older pastors around the country. At the same time, he is relentlessly challenging the churches of India to unleash the incredible potential that lies in young men and women to lead disciplemaking ministries among the most unreached peoples.

Our commitment to younger leaders does not mean we have narrowed our end-product to reaching global youth. Rather, youth are the means we are using to reach the world. We recognize and affirm that God will use other age groups in significant ways to accomplish this. However, our commitment first and foremost as a movement is to the young, in order to reach the rest of the world. At times, that requires us to begin training and cultivating relationships with senior pastors and elders because in many cultures, respect for elders is vital. Also, in some cultures a stereotypical "youth group" is never an appropriate end, given the blessing of intergenerational ministry already present and the limited influence of Western culture. However, our over twenty years of history, coupled with the needs of the world, makes younger leaders our key strategy for global multiplication.

3. Local Ministries Multiplied

We are committed to multiplication in and through the local church as God's chosen vehicle to reach the world. At Sonlife, our first love and sole reason for functioning is the church. Everything we do is in and through the church. We are not interested in asking the church to join *our* agendas. Rather, we want to serve in apostolic roles *with* the church.

While God has used some organizations to see fruit by planning or joining massive crusades and campaigns where soccer stadiums are filled with people to hear evangelistic messages, that's not our calling. We are called to work with churches to penetrate their respective communities through the everyday life of the church and its members.

Last summer, our ministry in Eastern Europe ran 48 evangelistic camps in Czech Republic, 5 in Romania, 9 in Poland, 2 in Slovakia and 2 in Ukraine. Each camp was based out of a single local church ministry. This is all part of an intentional effort by our ministry partners to run the ministry in and through a local assembly, so as to set up the potential for long-term multiplication from what occurs in those week-long camps.

4. Global Movement Synergized

We are committed to partnering with like-minded churches and organizations to make a Great Commission, healthy church accessible to every person on the globe. We are not committed to growing the institution of Sonlife internationally. It's not our role to create ministry plans and strategies for other contexts. Rather, as God connects us with like-minded leaders and ministries, we want to come alongside them to make their God-given dreams a reality. As we partner with others, our desire is to help church leaders in every people group of the world understand disciplemaking.

For example, Sonlife is partnering with several missions agencies to train non-Western missionaries to go into frontier fields, equip church-planters and send out missionaries who will equip others. A large relief and development organization is exploring a partnership with Sonlife to collaboratively equip church leaders ministering among the poorest of the poor. Colleges and seminaries are dialoguing with us about incorporating our non-traditional venues for education with their preparation of men and women pursuing ministry. Churches, counseling organizations, denominations and parachurch organizations are also considering, with us, how we can finish the task at hand together.

These four values are the threads that run through Sonlife as a movement internationally. We want to ignite and support church planting movements around the globe. We want to do so interdependently with the rest of the church worldwide.

Summary

There is nothing more compelling than the Story of God. Jesus' life and ministry bring meaning to my journey. It is my prayer that God might use this book to bring renewed vision and purpose to your life and ministry—and that he might use it to further the Great Commission, the calling on all our lives.

Notes

[1]Frank Buechner, *Telling the Truth: The Gospel as Tragedy, Comedy, and Fairy Tale*, in *The Sacred Romance: Drawing Closer to the Heart of God*, by Brent Curtis and John Eldridge (Nashville: Thomas Nelson, 1997) 46.

[2]Howard Hendricks. *Leadership Journal* (Summer 1982).

[3]The organic process refers to the birth, growth and reproduction of living things, as opposed to a packaged, mechanical process used with material things; this is further addressed in Part III.

Part I Mission:

Make Disciples

Connecting Your Journey with the Story of God:
Disciplemaking in Diverse Contexts

Part I Overview

Just before ascending to heaven, Jesus gives the clearest mandate of what should consume our lives—so we will begin by revisiting Christ's mandate, the Great Commission.

> Then Jesus came to them [the eleven disciples] and said, "All authority in heaven and on earth has been given to me. Therefore go and make disciples of all nations, baptizing them in the name of the Father and of the Son and of the Holy Spirit, and teaching them to obey everything I have commanded you. And surely I will be with you always, to the very end of the age" (Matt. 28:18-20.

The mountain top where Jesus and the disciples met was a place they had visited countless times. Jesus had often prayed there. It was probably the same mountain where Jesus brought James, John and Peter to worship him in his blazing, white glory.

Imagine them staring at the Sea of Galilee below. There were only eleven of them now. What must have gone through their minds? They watched the brutal murder of their friend and leader, Jesus, yet now he was alive. Or was he?

On one point they were very clear. There was no question he was King of the Jews. Having triumphed over evil and the cross, it probably didn't surprise them to hear him begin his final words by saying, "All authority in heaven and on earth has been given to me."

Make Disciples of All Nations

In the Greek text, the main command of the Great Commission is to "make disciples of all nations." To do so requires many people to uproot from their homelands. However, Jesus' primary focus is upon the task to reproduce ourselves wherever we are. To make a disciple is to bring one into a student/teacher relationship with Christ, accepting who Jesus is and submitting to his lordship. Disciples are those who hear, understand and obey Jesus' claims and teaching. We are to reproduce ourselves—disciples of Jesus Christ. So the command goes beyond simply making converts.

All nations refers not as much to geopolitical boundaries as it does to groups of people who share a common culture and/or language. Jesus' use of the word "nations" is better understood today by the contemporary term "people group," the largest possible group within which the gospel can spread as a movement without hitting barriers of misunderstanding. So Jesus says, "Go and make disciples of all the ethnic groups."

Jesus commissioned them as if they could see every single nation from the mountain top on which they stood. To disciple each one of the nations meant there would be a total transformation among every one of the tribes, languages and peoples. "They were commissioned to bring about a result, a response, a global following of Jesus from every people."[1]

Disciplemaking is more than what modern evangelicalism has called "discipleship." Certainly our contemporary notions of discipleship are part of disciplemaking but all too often, ministries conceive of discipleship as one program or aspect of church life. Disciplemaking encompasses everything we should be about in the church. It is the whole process of spiritual formation from lostness to being a fully devoted follower of Christ.

Jesus sent out his apostles to gather the scattered "sons of God" (John 11:52), and to "call the ransomed from every tongue and tribe and people and nation" (Rev. 5:9), until redeemed persons from "all the peoples praise him" (Rom. 15:11). Put simply, our responsibility is to make disciples of all people everywhere, without distinction. His last command is our first priority!

Notes

[1]S.C. Hawthorne, "Mandate on the Mountain," in *Perspectives on the World Christian Movement*, ed. R. Winter and S. Hawthorne (Pasadena, CA: William Carey Library, 1999), 110.

CHAPTER TWO

Great Commission Priorities:
Process and Vehicles for Disciplemaking

When Christ gave the command to make disciples, he included the process for doing so. Of course, this is what he had modeled for three years, but he summed it up in these final words. We will look at an overview of that process in the first half of this chapter and will then dig much deeper into each phase of this process in the chapters found in Part II. The second part of this chapter deals with the God-ordained vehicles for carrying out this process of disciplemaking.

The Process of Disciplemaking

Jesus commissioned his disciples to make disciples of all nations by going, baptizing and teaching. Look at what is meant by each of these.

Go: *Pursue contact with lost people.*

As already stated, the assumption is that we make disciples first and foremost in the culture of which we're a part. It is ingrained as part of our everyday lifestyle. "As you are going," it can be interpreted, "make disciples!" Further, the assumption is that a maturing disciple will consider his/her personal role in making disciples of all nations. Jesus mandated and modeled intentionally seeking the lost as part of making disciples. He multiplied this priority to his disciples as he sent them out to evangelize.

WIN

Throughout Christ's last three years of ministry, he modeled systematically ministering to specific regions (Mark 1:38; Matt. 4:23-25). He and his disciples had gone to different groups of people and intentionalized significant relationships to foster a lasting movement of the kingdom.

This was not a new theme for God's people. God had been planting the seeds for spreading his movement into other people groups all throughout history. Abram was the forerunner of those called to uproot his family to follow God's plan. God's promise to Abram was foundational to making disciples of all nations:

> The Lord had said to Abram, "Leave your country, your people and your father's household and go to the land I will show you. I will make you into a great nation and I will bless you; I will make your name great, and you will be a blessing. I will bless those who bless you, and whoever curses you I will curse; and all the peoples on earth will be blessed through you" (Gen. 12:1-3).

Intentionalize is a word and concept to which we will return many times throughout this book. Many ministries are doing good things, but are not being purposeful about it. The importance of *intentionality* comes from the text here in Matthew as well as from the model of Christ's life and ministry.

Baptize: *Identify believers with the person and work of Christ.*

John the Baptist baptized people as an identification of repentance from a former way of living and readiness to participate in the fullness of God and his kingdom. People had declared their repentance and readiness to follow the coming Messiah. Now Jesus was commissioning his disciples to baptize. The Messiah had come and every believer could encounter the Father through the Son. Baptism continued as a public identification with the body and work of Christ.

Baptism is an external expression that states, "I belong to Christ." Many cultures have symbols which communicate that one is married. In the United States, the gold band on my left hand says "Hands off! I belong to Linda!" My father never wore a wedding band because it irri-

Many ministries are doing good things, but are not being purposeful about it. The importance of intentionality comes from the text here in Matthew as well as from the model of Christ's life and ministry.

tated his skin. His ringless finger did not change the fact that he was married and committed to my mom. However, with the symbol missing, people sometimes falsely assumed he was unmarried. In a similar way, I believe conversion happens apart from baptism, but baptism publicly expresses belief in and commitment to Christ. It says, "I belong to Christ!" Baptism is a way of pledging allegiance, both to God and to the body of Christ.

Teach: *Equip believers to be active in the faith through serving God.*

Disciplemaking must be holistic. Clearly Jesus didn't intend for his disciples to merely disseminate their knowledge into their converts. He equipped them in the skills needed to carry on the ministry in his absence. His life was a model of how to live and what to do as he taught them how to function in all areas of life and ministry (Exod. 18:20). He expected his disciples to do the same as they made disciples. They were to teach followers of Christ to observe all he commanded them to do.

Jesus commissioned his disciples to make disciples by intentionalizing relationships with lost people (win) and by identifying people with the work of Christ (build). Further, they were to equip followers of Christ to know and follow him in the fullest way he could be known, that they might better make him known to others (equip to win).

The Vehicles for Disciplemaking

Throughout biblical history there have been distinct yet related models of ministry among the people of God. During the time of the Pentateuch, the family surfaces as the predominant context for redemptive activity. In the Poetic literature, sages and mentors with practical and heart-felt words of wisdom play a primary role. The Prophets use a confrontational approach with the rebellious nation of Israel. Jesus' incarnation emphasizes a ministry and message of making disciples through multiplication. Christ's ministry was further multiplied by the institution of the church throughout the Epistles. In all these phases, God has continually used leaders within two institutions—the community of believers and the family—to advance his plan. Let's look at those two institutions as God intends them, coupled with God's use of leaders in making disciples.

The Church

**Vehicles for
Disciplemaking**

The Church

Throughout the Old Testament, the people of God are juxtaposed against the rest of the world. We read about the ongoing tension between Israel and the Gentiles. As the people of Judah continue to rebel, God begins to reveal that only a remnant will truly remain as his people. Though only a remnant, they continue as a powerful force throughout history, their growth eventually including the grafting in of Gentile believers.

Since the Great Commission, the community of believers has existed within the institution of the church. The church is intended to assist believers in fulfilling the Great Commission. I love the church. I don't question that it has often missed the mark in fulfilling its mission, nor that it has often become an irrelevant institution. At the same time, the church, through its members, has brought about more change for the kingdom than any other institution. The only way I can reconcile ministering full-time in an organization outside the church is to be with an organization like Sonlife, where the local church is our lifeline. We exist for the church and for no other reason.

Authentic, New Testament disciplemaking is impossible without involvement in a local church. The final goal is not one's individual spirituality and relationship to God—it is the mutual and corporate growth of the whole body for the glory of God. Most of the New Testament references to spiritual maturity (Greek word *telios*) refer to a plural audience (Rom. 12:1-2; 1 Cor. 13:9; Phil. 3:15; Col. 1:28; 4:12; Heb. 5:14; 1 Pet. 2:2; 2 Pet. 3:18; 1 John 4:12). Spiritual growth occurs interdependently. You have been given spiritual gifts so that I can grow and I have been given spiritual gifts so that you can grow. My own spiritual development is important, but it's not the end. It is a means to corporate maturity, which brings the greatest honor and glory to God.

I frequently interact with youth ministry majors at Christian colleges and I am frightened to talk to so many who have little desire to minister within a local church. As I speak with aspiring missionaries, many seem far more energized by building institutions overseas that circumvent the church rather than working in and through the church as the ultimate tool. All too often, missions organizations have redefined missions wherein churches have become subservient to agencies and their agendas rather than visa versa. Sadly, I often encounter Christian leaders outside North America who emulate these same anti-church sentiments. Undoubtedly there are many reasons for Christian leaders' frustrations with the church, not the least of which is their own bad experiences; however, we must renew a love for the local church and champion it as God's chosen vehicle for assisting believers in making disciples.

I recently spoke at a church whose leadership proudly affirmed to me their success as a ministry. I asked them why they considered themselves successful. They began by giving me their short, pithy mission statement and they showed me their innovative technology. They told me all the conferences they have attended, referred to their pastor as the CEO, and talked to me about all the cutting edge music being used. I asked my question again saying, "That's interesting. But what is it that makes you feel like you're successful as a church?" They gave me an uncomfortable stare and reiterated the same things in a little different fashion.

I have no problem with the use of technology, the value of mission statements and diverse genres of worship. However, I am troubled by the consumeristic, businesslike mindset pervasive in so many of our churches. Matthew emphasizes the result of Jesus' ministry as the creation of a new community of the believing and forgiving remnant. Jesus depicts a vision for the church as a visible community of salt and light. In most parts of the world, the church finds itself in a post-Christian environment. D. L. Donaldson writes,

> The church, in fact, needs to see itself as Matthew saw it: as a distinct and appealing counterculture; a city set on a hill, making visible the reality of God's reign in the midst of the old

order; a community concerned not so much to root out the weeds in its midst as to cultivate wheat of such quality that others will see it "and give glory to your Father in heaven" (Matt. 5:16).[1]

As I interact with church leaders in the developing world, I become frustrated in not knowing how to help them be a visible community of salt and light amidst the vast crises of poverty and disease in so many of their cultures. In response, Sonlife and a large Christian relief and development organization are prayerfully pursuing a partnership. We want to jointly mobilize and equip church leaders to meet the full scope of needs facing most communities in the world. We want to help the church penetrate culture so that communities and nations are transformed. This is all part of making disciples of all nations through the vehicle of the church.

Unfortunately, the church often has a reputation different from what Christ intended. For example, a minister who works with homeless and hurting people in Chicago describes the desperate state of a prostitute who could hardly bear to talk about her sordid life. She was trapped in a lifestyle that seemed to be her only means of survival. When the minister asked if she had ever thought of going to a church for help she responded, "Church! Why would I ever go there? I was already feeling terrible about myself. They'd just make me feel worse."[2] I am confident that was not the perception Jesus intended for the church in carrying out his mandate.

While we cannot purport that Jesus' mission and the church's mission are identical, they are clearly comparable and inseparable. Jesus announced and offered himself as the agent of redemption and the church is to proclaim, extend and apply what Jesus effected.

This frequently cited passage from the 1952 Kerr Lectures bears repeating again here:

> It is surely a fact of inexhaustible significance that what our Lord left behind him was not a book, nor a creed, nor a system of thought, nor a rule of life, but a visible community...he com-

The church is God's chosen vehicle for communicating a vision of grace. It exists to assist believers in fulfilling Christ's mandate to make disciples.

mitted the entire work of salvation to that community. It was not that a community gathered round an idea, so that the idea was primary and the community secondary. It was that a community called together by the deliberate choice of the Lord himself, and recreated in him, gradually sought—and is seeking—to make explicit who he is and what he has done. The actual community is primary; the understanding of what it is comes second.[3]

The church is God's chosen vehicle for communicating a vision of grace. It exists to assist believers in fulfilling Christ's mandate to make disciples.

The Family

I am forever grateful to my parents for rearing me in godliness from the time of my birth. Nothing has more influenced my life than experiencing my parents' disciplemaking efforts with me and others. I long to further their investment in me through my relationship with my best friend and wife, Linda, and with our two girls, Emily and Grace. Linda and I want to prioritize, with God, discipling our daughters.

The nuclear family is the other primary institution God has used among the redemptive community all throughout biblical history. The family institution began with Adam and Eve (Gen. 1:26-28; 2:18-25; 4:1; 5:1-2) and the home remained central throughout Hebrew culture. Along with the church, it is affirmed throughout the New Testament as a God-ordained institution for disciplemaking.

As in many parts of the world today, the Old Testament family was much broader than the immediate family of mother, father and children. There was a definite head of the house and the first son was next in line. The remaining members of the immediate family followed in the hierarchy and then there were extended family members, families of friends, and families of slaves. The basic source of identity was one's household. The family was designed for full participation and enjoyment of both privilege and responsibility. Full allegiance and commitment to one's family was a given.

Vehicles for Disciplemaking

The Church

The Family

Religious nurture, transmission of tradition, worship and even vocational preparation were all rooted in the home (Exod. 12:26-27; 13:7-8, 14-16; Deut. 4:9; 6:7, 20-25; Prov. 6:20-23; 13:1; 23:33-35). Parents told stories (Deut. 5:20ff), gave explanations (Exod. 13:8; 14:6) and answered children's questions (Exod. 12:26).[4]

Perhaps there has never been a time when the family institution has seen as much disarray as it has today. All over the globe, families are experiencing varying levels of decay. At the same time, people in most every part of the globe still readily acknowledge parents as the primary influence in an individual's life.

Even more primary to a family than a parent/child relationship is the marital relationship. Marriage gives us a picture of God's relationship with his people. God wants our marriages to reflect his character and priorities. The marriage relationship is the most powerful of relationships, and a marriage partner will either enhance or degrade the glory of his/her spouse.[5] I am forever grateful for God's gift in giving me my wife and best friend Linda. No one has more influenced me to know God and make him known to others than she has. We must view our spouses first and foremost as image-bearers of God, though fallen. For those of us who are married, I can think of no influence that will greater leverage our disciplemaking with our children and with others than the strength of our marriages.

The Old Testament regularly reminds parents to use every chance to make disciples of their children. In talking about the commands of God, and specifically about the importance of loving God wholeheartedly, Moses says, "Impress them on your children. Talk about them when you sit at home and when you walk along the road, when you lie down and when you get up" (Deut. 6:7).

We must protect and use the God-ordained institution of the family as a primary force in making disciples. Parents need to be equipped with skills to disciple their children. Families must be honored and empowered to make disciples as part of their daily lives. Ministries should not compete with but jointly work with families to make disciples.

We must protect and use the God-ordained institution of the family as a primary force in making disciples.

At the same time, Jesus and the New Testament writers center the role of the family within the family of the kingdom of heaven. The church is God's most important earthly institution and is the social agent that most significantly shapes and forms the character of Christians. Families and individuals gain a distinctive Christian identity through their participation in the church.

Churches and families must collaboratively follow Christ's mandate to make disciples who make disciples who make disciples. All efforts to make disciples must keep these two biblical institutions paramount. They are God's chosen vehicles to assist people in disciplemaking.

The Leader

Throughout God's Story, the church and the family are the consistent institutions used by God, and chosen leaders are the consistent players used within these institutions. Adam, Noah, Abraham, Isaac, Jacob, Joseph, Samuel, David, Solomon, Nehemiah, Deborah, Isaiah and Jeremiah are but a few, albeit some of the most notable leaders among families and Judah in the Old Testament. John the Baptist, Jesus, Peter, Paul, John, James, Lois, Eunice and Timothy are some of the church and family leaders found in the New Testament. Then there are people like John Calvin, Martin Luther, John Wesley, Jonathan Edwards, Billy Graham and Bill Hybels, who have been used by God in these institutions over the last several hundred years. We could easily devote several volumes of books to God's use of leaders like these throughout his Story. However, since this book looks primarily at Jesus and his role as a ministry leader, I want to limit my analysis of leadership to looking at him.

Vehicles for Disciplemaking

The Church

The Family

Through the Leader

This book is devoted to studying Christ's leadership, so Christ will be our reference point for how to lead disciplemaking ministries throughout. In the next chapter, we will look at the foundational values that consistently characterized Jesus as a leader. We will review how his words and actions came from his love for the Father and his love for others.

God consistently uses other institutions and players to advance his kingdom. However, all throughout history we see the family and the church as the consistent vehicles that drive the process of his Story. Disciplemaking leaders must hold those institutions as paramount and must keep in perspective their part in the grander Story of which they are part.

Summary

Jesus commanded us to make disciples. But how? He told us that, too. Go! Baptize! Teach! That is, Win! Build! Equip! As disciplemaking leaders, we are to carry out that process in the God-given vehicles of the church and family.

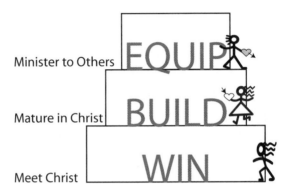

Minister to Others

Mature in Christ

Meet Christ

Notes

[1]D.L. Donaldson, "Guiding Readers—Making Disciples: Discipleship in Matthew's Narrative Strategy," in *Patterns of Discipleship in the New Testament*, ed. R. Longenecker (Grand Rapids: Eerdmans, 1996), 48.

[2]Philip Yancey, *What's So Amazing About Grace?* (Grand Rapids: Zondervan, 1997), 11.

[3]*The Household of God* (New York: Friendship Press, 1954), 20.

[4]Robert Banks, *Reenvisioning Theological Education: Exploring a Missional Alternative to Current Models* (Grand Rapids: Eerdmans, 1999), 106.

[5]Dan Allender, *Intimate Allies* (Wheaton, IL: Tyndale, 1995) 27.

CHAPTER THREE

Great Commandment Values:
The Personal Life of a Disciplemaker

Jesus said that the most important command is to love God and love others. Jesus' nature as a loving person is obvious throughout his life and ministry. He did not draw people by force, nor did he manipulate them with his power. Instead, grace, coupled with truth, was the over-whelming nature of his leadership (John 1:14). His grace unquestion-ably came out in aggressive ways at times, but never at the expense of all his other characteristics as God. In his approach to ministry, Christ's love for the Father and for others are all-consuming. If we fail to begin our disciplemaking journey with this same heart, it is unlikely we will produce Christ-followers. Love for God and others is the driving moti-vation behind making disciples.

> Jesus replied, "'Love the Lord your God with all your heart and with all your soul and with all your mind.' This is the first and greatest commandment. And the second is like it: 'Love your neighbor as yourself.' All the Law and the prophets hang on these two commandments" (Matt. 22:37-40).

By studying the Gospels, we find Christ built a foundation by em-phasizing a balance of loving God and loving others (the Great Com-mandment). His love for God and others can be expressed through six values that flowed through his life. We will look at these briefly now and watch them resurface later as we look at the Story of Christ's life and ministry.

There are at least six values from the Great Commandment which are consistently evident in Christ's life and ministry:

Loving God

1. Prayerful Dependence

2. Clear Understanding of Christ

3. Priority of God's Word

Loving Others

4. Building Intentional Relationships

5. Demonstrating Love

6. Clarifying Mission

Obviously, these six values don't fall exclusively under these two categories of loving God and loving others. As I demonstrate love for people in my ministry, I am loving God. As I pray dependently, that's an expression of love to people in my life. However, the distinction may help you remember the primary direction of each value. Christ embodied these values from his childhood through his crucifixion and beyond. Because these values were embraced by him as a leader, they overflowed into his ministry.

1. Prayerful Dependence

Time alone with the Father was central to every aspect of Christ's life and ministry. He frequently withdrew to be alone with the Father (Luke 5:16). In more than 45 sections of Scripture on 30 different occasions, Christ modeled and taught about prayer during his three-and-a-half years of ministry on earth. As the intensity of Christ's ministry grew, so did his priority of time with the Father.

Christ's disciples realized the significant role of prayer in their master's life. They said, "Lord, teach us to pray" (Luke 11:1). The disciples saw first hand, more than anyone else, that Jesus, in his humanity, viewed prayer as his pipeline to the heavenly Father.

S.D. Gordon writes,

> The great people of the earth today are the people who pray. I do not mean those who talk about prayer; nor those who say they believe in prayer; nor yet those who can explain about prayer; but I mean those people who take time to pray. …These are the people today who are doing the most for God; in winning souls; in solving problems; in awakening churches…[1]

2. Clear Understanding of Christ

The Messiah was expected to be a conquering king. Instead, he showed up as a suffering man from the working class. Christ's disciples gradually began to see Jesus for who he was, rather than trying to force him to be the Messiah they had expected. However, it took a number of experiences and two to three years for them to get to this point.

Jesus knew that only as people understood who he was and why he came would they begin to have the right motivation for following him. He spent more than two and a half years of his public ministry communicating primarily who he was and what he was going to do. He did this relationally and through his teaching times. Not until after the Twelve were chosen, commissioned and sent out did Christ gradually begin to emphasize the cost of following him. Dann Spader writes,

> It is clear that Jesus faced a generation that was looking for a triumphant, political savior. They wanted a powerful king riding a white horse, but he came as a suffering servant astride an awkward donkey. He simply didn't fit the mold that had been publicly predetermined for him. Yet a right relationship with him could only be based on accurate knowledge of who he was. This need was so great that much of his early ministry was specifically devoted to helping his disciples understand his identity. In fact, throughout the course of his entire ministry, he never ceased working on this issue.[2]

When Christ came in the form of a servant, he was not disguising who God is—he *revealed* who God is.[3]

3. Priority of God's Word

The Gospels show us at least eighty times when Christ refers to the Old Testament, quoting from over seventy different chapters. He knew the Word and used it regularly. It was the primary focus of his life and ministry.

He used it for his own learning (Luke 2:46), to resist Satan (Luke 4:1-13), and in his decision-making (Matt. 4:13-15). The Word guided Christ's priorities (Mark 1:38) and was his primary tool in responding to criticism (Matt. 9:13; Luke 13; John 10). He used the Word to train his disciples (Matt. 5), to commission the Twelve (Matt. 10:35-36), and even in his last hours on the cross (Matt. 27:46).

The early church followed Jesus' example and "devoted themselves to the apostles' teaching" (Acts 2:42). The leaders prioritized the Word by giving "attention to prayer and the ministry of the Word" (Acts 6:4).

4. Building Intentional Relationships

The most basic and profound priority of Jesus' approach was his focus on relationships. Nothing better demonstrates this than the Incarnation itself. Rather than download data about himself to people, God became a man through his Son, Jesus Christ. God himself became flesh and dwelt among us.

But even after he came to earth, as Jesus ministered, he spent very little time in the temple. He took the initiative to build relationships with people in their everyday life settings. His time traveling with the disciples, his attendance at the Cana wedding, and his conversation with the woman at the well all demonstrate ways Jesus lived out the value of relating to people.

Jesus' approach was remarkably simple. He didn't develop complicated schedules of membership classes nor did he write up a syllabus for a course of study. Jesus made a practice of spending purposeful time with people—he drew people to himself.

5. Demonstrating Love

Jesus' approach was so different from the contemporary leaders of his time because he didn't use power to coerce people to follow him; he drew them with love. In response to the leper, "filled with compassion, Jesus reached out his hand and touched the man" (Mark 1:41). When Jesus encountered the widow who had just lost her only son, Luke tells us, "When the Lord saw her, his heart went out to her and he said, 'Don't cry.'" (Luke 7:13). As he traveled among the crowds, we're told that he had "compassion on them" (Matt. 9:36) and wept over the blindness of the people in Jerusalem (Luke 19:41-42).

Many people in our ministries experience a never-ending barrage of attacks in school or at the work place, in their communities and sometimes even at home. One thing people should immediately find different about our ministries is an atmosphere of love. Our most powerful testimony to the world will be love (John 13:34-35). No one more influences the "love temperature" in a ministry than the leader personally.

Jesus both expresses his love for his disciples and commands them to imitate him by loving each other. He doesn't command them to love others until he first demonstrates his love for them (John 15:12-17).

Lawrence Richards writes that the overwhelming testimony of the New Testament is that:

> Love expressed and experienced among members of the body is absolutely essential if that body is to be healthy and alive… Thus the development of love within the body must be the primary concern of spiritual leaders.[4]

6. Clarifying Mission

Jesus didn't want his ministry known first and foremost by his miracles. Remember all the times he told those he healed to not tell anyone what he had just done? Why? Because he didn't want people to miss the real point.

Though Christ met people where they were, he continually challenged them to a higher calling. He was continually casting a sense of anticipation of what God desired to do in and through them. He wanted to get at the heart, not at what was merely on the outside. Look how John describes one of Christ's challenges to his followers:

> Jesus answered, "I tell you the truth, you are looking for me, not because you saw miraculous signs but because you ate the loaves and had your fill" (John 6:26).

> From this time many of his disciples turned back and no longer followed him. "You do not want to leave too, do you?" Jesus asked the Twelve. Simon Peter answered him, "Lord, to whom shall we go? You have the words of eternal life. We believe and know that you are the Holy One of God" (John 6:66-69).

Christ did not waiver in his mission. Everything he did flowed from his mission to make disciples who make disciples who make disciples. He challenged his followers to embrace that mission as well.

Summary

These were the values that guided Christ's behavior. His every word, thought and act flowed from these values of loving the Father and loving people. These priorities characterized his leadership and ministry. As Christ's ministry proceeded, "He was alone much of the time, often spending the entire night in solitude and prayer before serving the needs of his disciples and hearers the following day," writes Dallas Willard.[5] These foundational values allowed Christ to lead a public life of ministry. Willard continues:

> He was able to love his closest companions—even though they often disappointed him greatly and seemed incapable of entering into his faith and works. And then he was able to die a death unsurpassed for its intrinsic beauty and historical effect.[6]

As God calls and allows us to lead disciplemaking ministries, we must emulate the Great Commandment lifestyle Christ used within the two institutions designed for making disciples—the church and the family. We must live as he lived in all of life, emulating his overall lifestyle. As we do so, we can expect to see the Father have his way in our lives and ministries just as he did in Christ's.

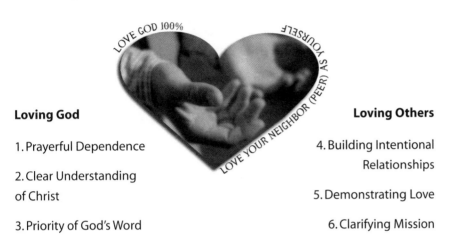

Loving God

1. Prayerful Dependence

2. Clear Understanding of Christ

3. Priority of God's Word

Loving Others

4. Building Intentional Relationships

5. Demonstrating Love

6. Clarifying Mission

Notes

[1] S.D. Gordon, *Quiet Talks on Prayer* (New York: Revell, 1904), 12.

[2] Gary Mayes and Dann Spader, *Growing a Healthy Church* (Chicago: Moody Press, 1991), 79.

[3] John Ortberg, *The Life You've Always Wanted* (Grand Rapids: Zondervan, 1997), 106.

[4] Lawrence Richards, *A Theology of Church Leadership* (Grand Rapids: Zondervan, 1980).

[5] Dallas Willard, *The Spirit of the Disciplines: Understanding How God Changes Lives* (New York: Harper Collins, 1988), 5.

[6] Ibid.

CHAPTER FOUR

End Results:
Objectives for Disciplemaking

The process of disciplemaking is not an end in and of itself. It is intended to produce disciples who produce other disciples. In addition, the Story of God shows us that disciplemaking should produce healthy, balanced ministries which transform their communities and nations, which ultimately brings increased glory to God.

It is important to take time to define these end results for our ministries. The degree to which we can clearly define what we're trying to produce is the degree to which we can fine tune our strategy for making disciples. It is also the degree to which we can effectively evaluate whether or not we are accomplishing our objectives.

Good gardeners have clearly defined pictures of what they intend to produce even before cultivating the soil. Knowing that the end product is going to be a plump and juicy tomato or a brilliant, beautiful rose motivates the gardener to nurture the growth of a plant in certain ways. Every plant must go through the same essential process of fertilization, initial growth, pruning, increased growth, weeding, etc. No two tomatoes or roses will look exactly the same, but there are definite characteristics determining whether or not the gardening process has been a success.

In a similar way, coaches have an end result in mind when working with a player. They will not try to make every player the same but good coaches will have clearly defined characteristics they will attempt to foster in each player.

Defining end results does not imply a fabrication of mechanically-produced products. We're not after an assembly line approach to manufacturing disciples. Rather, we must discern the desired characteristics for those going through the organic process of disciplemaking, acknowledging the diversity involved in each person and context, but also understanding the common characteristics of fruitfulness.

Disciplemaking endeavors should produce fully devoted disciples of Christ who are part of healthy, balanced ministries which transform their communities all for the glory of God. I have briefly described what is meant by each of these. They are fleshed out in greater detail in the following chapters.

Fully Devoted Disciples of Christ

At the heart of disciplemaking ministry is the desire to produce believers who reflect the character and priorities of Christ. Fully trained disciples are capable of and motivated to reach and care for people—they make disciples who make disciples who make disciples. The kind of followers we want to produce demonstrate ongoing growth and maturity. Mature disciples never see a task that appears "beneath" them, yet we cannot consider disciples as mature if we don't see them reproducing their lives in the lives of others who cross their paths.

Healthy, Balanced Ministries

Seeker-driven? Cell-based? Word-centered? Worship-focused? What's the ideal for a church and its ministries? One looking at the plethora of books and seminars around the world that address church leadership could easily be diverted in any number of directions. Which one is best? Which one is right? We must lead churches that reflect all the priorities of Christ's mandate. If the process is to go (win), baptize (build) and teach (equip) in order to make disciples, then our ministries must incorporate all these priorities.

A healthy ministry moves believers toward maturity in Christ (Col. 1:28-29) through teaching, fellowship, prayer, mutual care and concern and praise and worship (Acts 2:42-47). In addition, a healthy ministry equips mature believers to minister to others. Ministry to others takes two forms. First, exercising spiritual gifts within the body of Christ for edification, and second, exercising gifts outside the body of Christ to share Christ with lost people (Eph. 4:11-16). A healthy ministry assists believers in reaching out to lost people and it helps church members succeed in using their spiritual gifts.

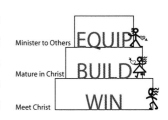

Transformed Communities and Nations

Academic institutions develop initiatives to foster learning throughout the community. Numerous organizations teach literacy, while others collect food and clothing for the needy. The local museum exhibits some of the best art created in recent days. The city compels people to care for the environment. Special interest groups rally concern for racism. All too often I look at agendas like these and ask, "Where is the church in all this?"

At times our ministries are caught up with saving souls at the expense of redeeming the rest of the culture. I'm not suggesting we should add political agendas and every social concern to our strategic plans, but when a church truly functions like a church should, it is the predominant force of good in its respective community. In fact, I am confident there is no force in the world with the potential strength of the local church. Nobody is better situated to respond to AIDS, illiteracy, poverty, disaster, single parenting, child abuse and other social concerns than the church. Sadly, some communities with the highest concentration of churches experience some of the greatest intensity of these problems.

Without question, the greatest need in the world is forgiveness of sins. Yet many times meeting that need requires a more holistic approach to redemption. God's Story speaks to matters such as salvation, baptism, prayer and the church to be sure; but it also speaks to everything in our life and world, including technology, economics and service. The Fall affected creation in every way and the redemption of Christ reaches just as far as the Fall. Albert Wolters writes, "To conceive of either the fall or Christ's deliverance as encompassing less than the whole of creation is to compromise the biblical teaching of the radical nature of the Fall and the cosmic scope of redemption."[1]

As individuals and ministries reflect the character and priorities of Christ, the overflow is evident in culture. Let us not forget the breadth of influence the Great Commission can have when fully exercised.

The Glory of God

John Piper writes, "Missions exists because worship doesn't."[2] Ultimately, the point of God's Story is not missions, it's not salvation, it's not families and it's not disciplemaking. The point of God's Story is God!

> The most crucial issue in missions is the centrality of God in the life of the church. Where people are not stunned by the greatness of God, how can they be sent with the ringing message, "Great is the Lord and greatly to be praised; he is to be feared above all gods"? (Ps. 96:4).[3]

When all is said and done, we are not the point; God is. "For my own sake, for my own sake, I do this. How can I let myself be defamed? I will not yield my glory to another." (Isa. 48:11). The greatest result of making disciples like Jesus did is the glory it brings to God.

Summary

So we're to go (win people to Christ), baptize (build up believers in the faith) and teach them to obey (equip believers to do ministry). We're to do so using the primary vehicles God has given, the family and the church. As leaders, we must make the Great Commandment values foundational in our lives and in our reaching out to others. The end-product includes Christ followers in healthy, balanced ministries who transform communities and nations for the glory of God. That end-product is the measuring stick for everything else done in life and ministry.

Notes

[1]Albert Wolters, *Creation Regained: Biblical Basics for a Reformational Worldview* (Grand Rapids: Eerdmans, 1988) 71.

[2]John Piper, *Let the Nations be Glad: The Supremacy of God in Missions* (Grand Rapids: Baker Books, 1993), 11.

[3]Ibid.

Part I Conclusion

Some people have moving stories about last words from loved ones, just before losing them to eternity. I lost my dad unexpectedly last summer. I called him in the morning to tell him we had just given him another granddaughter. By the time I got home from the hospital that evening, my mom called to tell me my dad had suddenly slipped into eternity. Regretfully, I don't have any special last words to which I can cling. In contrast, Christ's last words summed up the single mission of his life: "Make disciples." Was he hitting his disciples with these words for the first time, just before taking off to return to heaven? Did this sound entirely foreign to them? I don't think so. After all, this had been fore-shadowed all throughout the Old Testament, from as far back as Genesis. The Gospels show Jesus gradually but proactively moving his disciples toward the type of ministry he was now commissioning them to do. Christ's prejudice-free ministry among Samaritans and Gentiles, coupled with the way he intentionalized his three years of ministry had given them a real-life demonstration of how to carry out the mandate. Further, if they obeyed, he added the promise of his own authority and presence and just after he ascended to heaven, he added the further promise of the Holy Spirit (Acts 1:8).

Now let's take a closer look at what led up to Jesus' last words, the Great Commission, and what followed. I challenge you to consider the implications for your life and ministry. Stop and ask God to stretch your understanding of his Story. Ask him to engage you with his Master Plan as you seek to connect your ministry plan with it.

Part II Process:

Jesus' Life and

Ministry

Connecting Your Journey with the Story of God:
Disciplemaking in Diverse Contexts

Part II Overview

The pages which follow are intended to engage us in the story of Jesus' ministry and to consider the timeless ingredients that can transform our lives and ministries.[1]

We want to deeply engage in the life of Jesus. We want to *deconstruct*[2] what he did. What did he do when? Why? What resulted? How would he do it today? What would be the same? What would be different? How does my life and ministry connect with the Story? As we wrestle with these questions, we want to work at reconstructing the Story and finding our place in it. Our lives and ministries continue the Story and Program of God. As we revisit the familiar events in Christ's life, we want to read them with a lens that looks for Christ's approach to ministry. We want to be moved anew by the engaging person of Christ while also learning ministry from him.

Robert Coleman writes:

> The Master disclosed God's strategy of world conquest. That is why it is so important to observe the way Jesus maneuvered to achieve His objective. He had confidence in the future precisely because he lived according to that plan in the present. There was nothing haphazard about His life—no wasted energy nor an idle word. He was on business for God (Luke 2:40). He lived, He died, and He rose again according to schedule. Like a General plotting His course of battle, the Son of God calculated to win. He could not afford to take a chance. Weighing every alternative and variable factor in human experience, He conceived a strategy that would not fail.
>
> That strategy is worth careful consideration. It is tremendously revealing to study it. Serious reflection at this point will bring the student of Christ to some profound and perhaps shattering conclusions, though the realization will likely be slow and arduous. In fact, at first glance it might even appear that Jesus had no strategy.

Another approach might discover some particular technique but miss the underlying pattern of it all. This is one of the marvels of His strategy. It is so unassuming and silent that it is unnoticed by the hurried churchman.

But when the realization of his controlling method finally dawns on the open mind of the disciple, he will be amazed at its simplicity and wonder how he could have ever failed to see it before. Nevertheless, when His plan is reflected upon, the basic philosophy is so different from that of the modern church that its implications are nothing less than revolutionary.[3]

Luke writes a chronological account of Christ's life and ministry (Luke 1:3), so his Gospel serves as our basic timeline for studying Christ's process of ministry. Stop and ask God to help you engage in the Story of Jesus in a fresh way. Ask the Spirit to illuminate it to you in a manner that transforms your life and ministry.

Notes

[1]I have strived to develop this material with a multicultural team rather than seeking to imperialize local church ministry based upon my own cultural interpretation of the Bible.

[2]I am using the word "deconstructing" here to describe our need to analyze and unpack the life and ministry of Christ in a way that goes beyond our preconceived notions and assumptions. This is *not* used in association with Deconstructionism, which approaches a text with no regard for the author's original intent.

[3]Robert Coleman, *The Master Plan of Evangelism* (Grand Rapids: Baker Books, 1993), 24-25.

CHAPTER FIVE

Pre-Incarnation and Growing Up Years
Luke 1:1 – 3:20

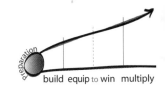

All too often we conduct a study of Christ by only looking at the New Testament. Christology must also examine the presence of the second person of the Trinity in the Old Testament. Messianic prophecies such as Genesis 3:15 (which speaks of the seed of the woman that will crush the serpent's head) reveal Christ as the hero of God's Story early on. Events like Christ's wrestling match with Jacob and his appearance to Isaiah give us other glimpses of the God-man. As the Story unfolds, with increasing clarity, we see God's purpose to redeem humanity through Jesus, all as part of his relentless plan to bring glory and honor to himself. We cannot fully learn from Jesus' approach to ministry without examining his presence long before his incarnation.

Christ plays a predominant role in creation. When we read, "God said, 'Let there be light,'" (Gen. 1:3a) we are hearing from Christ the Creator. John declares, "Through him all things were made; without him nothing was made that has been made" (John 1:3). Paul says "There is but one lord, Jesus Christ, through whom all things came and through whom we live" (1 Cor. 8:6), and "All things were created by him and for him. He is before all things, and in him all things hold together" (Col. 1:16b-17). Christ is the Creator, Preserver and Goal of all creation!

Christ is called Jehovah in the Old Testament. Jehovah "rained down burning sulfur on Sodom and Gomorrah" (Gen. 19:24). His role as Savior is often referenced too. "Yet I will show love to the House of

Judah; and I will save them—not by bow, sword, or battle, or by horses and horsemen, but by the Lord their God" (Hos. 1:7).

Most often, Christ appears in the Old Testament as the Angel of Jehovah, whose manifestation in angelic or human form foreshadowed his final coming in the flesh. In this role, he appears to Hagar to tell her to return and submit to Sarah (Gen. 16:7-14). He speaks to Abraham when Abraham is about to slay his long-awaited son Isaac (Gen. 22:11-18). Jacob is in the midst of Laban's unfair dealings when he hears from the Lord (Gen. 31:11, 13) and Moses experiences the coming Messiah in a burning bush (Exod. 3:2-5). Christ, the second Person of the Trinity, has a distinct, personal presence that recurs throughout the Old Testament.

Abraham's faithful obedience to leave the pagan land of Ur lays the foundation for Christ's incarnation many centuries later. Jacob the conniver manipulates his way to his inheritance. However, he is forever changed when he encounters the God-man at Bethel. Striking similarities exist between Moses and Jesus, though Jesus outshines Moses in every way. Jesus' earliest days on earth look a lot like Moses' days as a baby, including the attempted annihilation of God's deliverer by killing off all boys their ages, as well as their exiles to Egypt. Moses was hunted by Pharaoh; Jesus was hunted by Herod. Read the narrative in Matthew 2 and consider God's divine preservation of the Savior of God's people, the new "Moses" of the new "exodus." The transfiguration, recorded in three of the four Gospels, overtly presents Jesus as the new Moses, though again, far outshining Moses' glory. "Moses was faithful as a servant in all God's house, testifying to what would be said in the future. But Christ is faithful as a son over God's house" (Heb. 3:5-6a).

Jesus is the true King in the line of David. It is therefore not surprising to see Jesus called "son of David" numerous times throughout the Gospels. David was a great man, but like the others, paled in contrast with the Perfect King. More is known about David than about any other individual in the Old Testament. As I read the first ten chapters of 2 Samuel, I marvel at David's leadership over Judah. In 2 Samuel 7, David looks around at the palace of cedar he calls home and is convicted that God doesn't have a house. God replies, "I appreciate the thought, David. But I want to build you a house that will last forever!" God thought enough of King David to bless his lineage so that the Messiah would come through him. David was a great man who wholeheartedly served God; and Christ was going to be his descendant! This is incredible!

The first ten chapters of 2 Samuel praise David's triumphs while the remaining chapters describe David's troubles. The consequences of David's lust, murder and cover-up follow him to the grave. When David finally repents, God speaks to him through Nathan (2 Sam. 12:7ff). God says, "David, I have given you everything. I have been as good as good could be, and if all this had been too little, I would have given you even more! That's how committed I am to you, David. That's how much I am on your side! I will forgive you, but you must live with the consequences of your sin for the rest of your life. You will see your family torn apart by hatred, murder and death. Lust will dominate your children, and what you did in private, they will do in public. And your son will die." From now on, David is a marked man for all to see.[1] In contrast, Christ comes several generations later and infinitely supersedes David as King. The fruit of Christ's flawless leadership is multiplied for eternity.

One of my favorite places to see Jesus appear in the Old Testament is through the prophet Isaiah. Isaiah writes sixty-six chapters to communicate a vision of grace. In the first five chapters, he speaks to Israel on God's behalf. He indicts them to reveal their need for grace. These are hard-hitting words. Isaiah calls Judah dumber than a jackass, and likens people to the people of Sodom and Gomorrah. He tells them God hates their worship. At the same time, Isaiah weaves hope all throughout the message of judgment. "Come now…your sins are like scarlet, but they shall be white as snow" (Isa. 1:18).

In the wake of King Uzziah's death, the self-dependent king who portrayed Judah's hardened heart, Isaiah sees another King to whom he must redirect Judah's attention. Isaiah is ushered into the very temple and presence of God, and Jesus himself is sitting on the throne. Christ's majesty overwhelms Isaiah as the seraphs fly and repeat, "Holy, holy, holy, is the Lord God Almighty; the whole earth is full of his glory" (Isa. 6:3). The temple is shaking and Isaiah responds, "Woe is me. I am ruined!" He is seeing the Messiah in all his glory (John 12:41). What a vision! Knowing his sinfulness, Isaiah presumes he will never get out alive. Jesus looks at one of the seraphs, nods, and has one of them put a hot coal on Isaiah's lips to atone him. Just when Isaiah thinks he's going to be dead, he's forgiven. God tells Isaiah, "Through sacrifice Isaiah, you can be forgiven." When asked, "Whom shall I send and who will go for us?" (Isa. 6:8), Isaiah immediately responds "Here am I, send me!"[2]

If I were Jesus, it would have been all I could do to restrain myself from saying, "Isaiah, I will be the sacrifice. I myself will come to earth in a few hundred years to fulfill this vision I am giving you." Jesus shows more restraint than that, but his grace shows no restraint. As we see Jesus for who he is, full of grace, all the conditions and restrictions are gone. Isaiah wants to be part of what he has seen and wants to share with others what he has experienced.

Even after Christ comes to earth, the majority of his time here is spent in preparation. We read a great deal about Jesus' entry and about his ministry, death and ascension, but the years in between remain somewhat obscure. We can be sure, though, that the first thirty years of his life are a time of personal preparation, growth and development (Luke 2:40). Even at age 12, Jesus is focused on his mission (Luke 2:41ff). His time of preparation culminates in the ministry of John the Baptist, who comes as one "preparing the way for the Lord." John presents Jesus as the person who will fulfill God's mission (Luke 3).

Dallas Willard says it well:

> We forget that being the unique Son of God clearly did not relieve him of the necessity of a life of preparation that was mainly spent out of the public eye. In spite of the auspicious events surrounding his birth, he grew up in the seclusion of a simple family in lowly Nazareth. At age 12, as Luke 2:46-47 tells us, he

exhibited astonishing understanding "sitting among the teachers" in Jerusalem. Yet he returned home with his parents and for the next eighteen years was subject to the demands of his family.[3]

Summary

Seeing Christ's role in the Trinity in the Old Testament reminds me of all he gave up to come to earth as a human. He humbles himself by becoming "nothing, taking the very nature of a servant, being made in human likeness" (Phil. 2:7). He is obedient even to the point of death!

Andrew Hodges writes a provocative, fictitious interview in his book, *Jesus: An Interview Across Time*. He suggests that Christ may not have been aware of his deity as a young boy. Might it be that Christ discovered that he is God at age eleven or twelve when he began to see himself and his life again and again in the Old Testament?[4] It's an intriguing consideration. What are the implications of the God-man being one hundred percent God and one hundred percent man?

Regardless, Christ was a rebel who, like many younger leaders today, questioned organized religion and reacted against the religious institutions of his time. His life was characterized most by loving God and loving others.

When Jesus begins his public ministry, he is well-prepared by having lived out the Great Commandment values. We can be sure that the Great Commandment values we see surfacing all throughout Jesus' ministry, were things he prioritized during these years prior to his public ministry (prayer, Christ, Word, relationships, love, mission).

Jesus draws people to himself because of who he is. Jesus' ministry is personal in nature at this point. People choose to follow him based upon his character and priorities.

As we begin ministry in a context, whether among unreached people or among a core of passionate followers of Jesus, we must begin by living the Great Commandment. As Christ does so in his context, some begin to believe. He challenges them to follow him.

Jesus' ministry is personal in nature at this point. People choose to follow him based upon his character and priorities.

Notes

[1]L. Konopka, "David's Watergate: I'm Pregnant" (Blythefield Hills Baptist Church, Rockford, MI, 22 March 1998).

[2]L. Konopka, "Communicating a Vision of Grace" (Blythefield Hills Baptist Church, Rockford, MI, 18 October 1998).

[3]Dallas Willard, *The Spirit of the Disciplines: Understanding How God Changes Lives* (New York: Harper Collins, 1988), 5.

[4]Andrew G. Hodges, *Jesus: An Interview Across Time* (New York: Bantam Books, 1986).

CHAPTER SIX

Building for Ministry
Luke 3:21 – 4:44

After thirty years of preparation for his ministry by prioritizing his love for the Father and for people, Christ began his public ministry. However, he didn't begin among the influential middle class and natural leaders in the political nerve centers of Rome or Jerusalem. Instead, we see him upriver in Galilee among the working class. He spent the first 18-20 months of his ministry here laying a foundation. His priority during this time was to build an environment that would stimulate spiritual growth. He did not focus on reaching the masses. Rather, he chose to build close relationships with a small group of people who would become his disciples. Though he didn't focus on evangelizing the masses, he did engage in personal evangelism. People were drawn to him and he challenged them to follow him. He only performed a few miracles and they were designed to reveal his identity to the people following him. This period began with Jesus' baptism and lasted until his rejection at Nazareth.

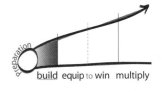

Baptism

Right after Jesus is baptized by John and God the Father says to him, "You are my Son, whom I love; with you I am well pleased" (Luke 3:22), the Spirit leads him to the desert, where the devil tempts the Messiah (Luke 4). The encounter with Satan was very real and the conflict was genuine. There's no question about that. Could Jesus have sinned? That's a difficult tension for sure, but we must most importantly remember that while Jesus was God, he was also fully man. He chose to veil his deity in order to fully express his humanity (Phil. 2).

Temptation

He, like you and me, had the ability to submit to the Father with the opportunity for the Father's power to flow through him. The temptation was real and significant, though I don't fully understand how his deity played into it. I must admit, sometimes I struggle to understand the evil in the three requests made by Satan—stone to bread, offering all the kingdoms of the world, and jumping from a high place. I'm tempted with things like lust, greed and discontentment. So why was Jesus tempted with all these abstract things? I'm not certain, but clearly something happened in the desert. Perhaps the greatest struggle for Jesus was putting up with Satan in the first place when he could have easily annihilated him. However, Jesus refuses to dazzle Satan the way Satan wants to be dazzled.

A couple years ago I was listening to a radio host interviewing and belittling a Christian author. The radio host said to his guest, "Okay, if your God is real and so powerful, have him throw me off the thousands of radio stations airing this program right now and zap me off my chair." I listened with anticipation. Nothing happened. A minute later, the radio host was boasting, "See, your God is afraid of me!" I began to think, "God, why didn't you do it!? What a statement that would have made." Of course he could have done it, but to have done so would have been to allow the radio host to determine how God should act. I, along with the radio host, was levying the same temptation to God that Jesus faced 2,000 years ago in the desert. Christ faces this same temptation countless more times during his earthly ministry, not the least of which is being taunted at the cross to call upon the angels to rescue him. Jesus' love for you and me and his commitment to build his ministry through grace rather than force is demonstrated right at the forefront of his public ministry.

First Followers

As Jesus returns from the desert, John the Baptist proclaims, "I am not the Christ" (John 1:20) and he affirms Jesus as the true Messiah. Jesus calls his first followers to "Come see," and five men follow him. Jesus' first miracle (John 2:1-11) takes place at the wedding in Cana. When his mother tells him the wine has run out, he tells his mother,

"My time has not yet come." However, Christ reveals his glory and his disciples take their first step of faith as he turns the water into wine.

After the wedding, Jesus, along with his mother, brothers and disciples, travel quite a distance to Capernaum just before the Passover (John 2:12ff). They spend a few days together there. Then Jesus goes down to Jerusalem and finds his Father's house turned into a market. He responds forcefully by driving out the animals from the temple area, scattering the money, turning over the tables and saying "How dare you turn my Father's house into a market!" Jesus does some additional miracles during this trip to Jerusalem and many more believe in him. However, Jesus isn't satisfied with a superficial faith that believes in him solely because of miracles; so he does not entrust himself to them.

Passover

During this first trip to Jerusalem, Nicodemus, an upper class leader who is interested in what Jesus has been doing, comes to interview him (John 3). As Nicodemus asks his questions, Jesus continues to tell him that citizenship in the kingdom of God cannot be achieved through a list of rules or outward conformity. He tells Nicodemus that one can only enter the kingdom as a result of a direct act of God. Jesus authoritatively describes himself as the One sent by God to save the world from condemnation.

Nicodemus

Jesus and his disciples go on from Jerusalem to the Judean countryside and baptize more followers. Meanwhile, John is baptizing with his disciples quite a distance up the Jordan River, and during a dispute between John's disciples and another Jew, John further affirms Jesus' deity.

As Jesus and his disciples head north back to Galilee, they go through Samaria, where that Jesus meets the Samaritan woman at the well in Sychar (John 4:4ff). The cultural norms of the day prohibited public conversation between men and women, particularly between Jews and Samaritans, and even between strangers. With that in mind, you can imagine the Samaritan woman's shock when Jesus asked her for a drink. After capturing her attention and piquing her curiosity, Jesus begins to talk with her about living water. It's as if Jesus is saying, "You think you're shocked that a strange Jewish man spoke to you. If you under-

Samaritan Woman

stood who I really am, you would be dumbfounded!" Jesus begins to reveal who he is to her and eventually tells her his full identity. Just then, the disciples rejoin Jesus and the woman runs into town to tell other Samaritans about who and what she had just experienced. As they come to hear from Jesus themselves, they say to the woman, "We no longer believe just because of what you have said; now we have heard for ourselves, and we know that this man really is the Savior of the world" (John 4:42).

As Jesus continued the trek to Galilee with his disciples, he talks to them about the privilege that is theirs to reap the harvest of crops planted by others before them. Jesus says, "Welcome to the harvest! You know the old saying, 'one sows and another reaps.' I sent you to reap what you didn't work for and you have reaped the benefits of others' hard labor." He essentially says, "Have a good time reaping the harvest, but don't get prideful. This isn't your crop. You're the reaper, but remember what generations before you tirelessly and thanklessly sowed. Without them, there would be no harvest. Don't forget it!" (John 4:3-38)

Jesus is welcomed as he enters Galilee and he preaches, "The kingdom of God is near. Repent and believe the good news!" (Mark 1:14b). He teaches in the synagogues, and news about him quickly spreads as he emphasizes repentance and faith. Jesus travels back over to Cana, heals the official's son (John 4:46-54), and then goes home to Nazareth (Luke 4:16ff). Despite his popularity elsewhere, he is rejected in his hometown. The people of Nazareth are filled with rage at the thought that Jesus would claim to be the Messiah. So Jesus leaves Nazareth and sets up home in Capernaum (Matt. 4:13-16).

Rejected at home

This period in Jesus' ministry lasts about one-and-a-half years. It's noteworthy that with only three years for his ministry, Jesus spends half of it establishing a foundation by calling followers and instilling in them the Great Commandment values from his own life.

- Go back through this chapter or read Luke 3-4 and see if you agree. Do you see the Great Commandment values evident in his life and ministry?

The Samaritan woman is surprised to find a Jewish man talking to her at all, and in her own "unclean" town at that. The Father overtly expresses his love for the Son and Jesus does the same with his followers. John the Baptist creates a sense of hope and expectancy for Jesus, and Jesus continues that among his followers. Jesus regularly prioritizes time alone with his Father to realign himself. Jesus declares to Nicodemus his divine identity and mission, and his understanding and use of the Word is already very apparent at this point in his ministry. These are but a few examples of how Jesus lives out the Great Commandment values which are so much a part of him.

Ministry Process

As Christ lives out the Great Commandment values in his life and ministry, he calls his followers to do the same. In observing Jesus' ministry and the ministry of his disciples that follows, the personal ownership of these Great Commandment values results in a priority of building believers both vertically (with God) and horizontally (with others). As an overflow of his personal life and mission, Jesus establishes key patterns for growth in the life of his followers. Acts 2 tells us the early church continues to practice these patterns. The Spirit uses the ownership of the Great Commandment values in the lives of leaders to produce ministry priorities which can be described as Word, worship, community and serving. As the disciples grow, their experiences in each of these areas grow as well. Look briefly at these areas.

Great Commission Priorities

1. Word

This priority refers not only to knowing the Scriptures but also to encountering the living Word of God and allowing the Spirit to mold us in accordance thereto (Matt. 4:17; Luke 4:16-31). Jesus studies, owns and lives out the Word of God in his life. However, he is also committed to helping others encounter the Word. Many people in ministry who are tired of trying to come up with more entertaining programs to ap-

Priorities

1. Word

pease their congregations conclude, "Just teach the Word!" Others react the other way and give up on engaging people in the Word and simply try to entertain them. Either extreme is inconsistent with what we see in Christ's ministry.

As we live out the Great Commandment values in our own lives and ministry, we must ask God to use that to bring us to a place where we can communicate the Word of God. When all is said and done, the Word, God's revelation of himself, is the most valuable thing we can give followers of Jesus.

2. Worship

Priorities

1. Word

2. Worship

This is our response to God. Jesus worships the Father by words, actions and approach to ministry. He continually draws attention back to the Father. He always gives his Father the glory for the miracles he does. Christ calls his followers to revere God in such a way that he is glorified by their thoughts and expressions. He is continually planting seeds in his followers for the development of this priority (Luke 3:21; John 2:11; John 4:23-24). As we and our followers wholly embrace the Great Commandment, worship is a natural response. We need outlets to do it together, including times of prayer, music, art and other creative venues for corporately exalting God. Prayerful dependence and a proper understanding of who Jesus is will lead us to prioritize time in our ministries to adore God.

Our ministries must look for diverse and creative ways to worship God. Worship captures all that we're to be about. We must work with the Spirit in creating opportunities for responding to what God has done.

3. Community

Priorities

1. Word

2. Worship

3. Community

This is the oneness Christ offers in place of the loneliness produced by sin. Jesus prioritizes time with other people committed to the Father and his kingdom (John 1:39; 2:12; 4:40). This ministry priority is a natural outgrowth of the value Jesus gives to expressing love and intentionalizing relationships. Notice how the Great Commandment values continue to surface in these four patterns of growth. Christ fostered community among his followers wherever he went.

Churches should be sharpening havens for believers. Christ-followers should feel like church is a place where they can come and authentically relate to one another with grace and truth. It should be a place where love is experienced and expressed. It should be the lifeline to believers' personal growth and ministry.

Our ministries must be characterized as communities called together around the person and priorities of Christ. Community, not institutionalism, has always been and will continue to be the visible and witnessing force in God's movement. Community reflects the very nature of God. It's a defining characteristic of what we can expect for all of eternity with the family of God and with God himself!

4. Serving

This refers to prioritizing time with others to the extent that we adjust our lifestyles to express care and meet needs. Jesus' attitude of serving surfaces early in the Gospels, and he provides opportunities for his followers to serve along with him (Matt. 11:5; John 2:1-11; 4:46-54). This was one of the marked differences between Jesus' leadership and the authoritarian approaches of his contemporaries.

Priorities

1. Word
2. Worship
3. Community
4. Serving

As God's spirit moves through a group, serving others will be a natural response. The Spirit uses our ministries to reach out to other people. Serving others requires a sensitivity to the needs of others to know how to meet their needs best. Again, there is an obvious connection between the Great Commandment values of intentionalizing relationships with others and expressing love with this ministry priority of serving.

Jesus' first 18-20 months of public ministry initiated ministry priorities which should be present in every disciplemaking ministry.

- Which of these priorities are you most inclined to emphasize/de-emphasize?
  ❏ Word ·   ❏ Worship   ❏ Community   ❏ Serving

CHAPTER SEVEN

Equipping Workers to Win the Masses
Luke 5:1 – 6:11

It's winter, A.D. 28. Jesus has just moved into the Galilee region, specifically Capernaum, after 18-20 months in the Judean wilderness area. He begins to intensify relationships with a few of his followers (Simon, Andrew, James and John—Mark 1:16-20) and he calls them to be involved with him in ministry as "fishers of men" (Matt. 4:19; Mark 1:17).

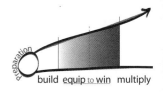

From this point on, most of the references to Jesus almost always include the phrase, "and the disciples." Often after a sermon, Jesus explains his message in a deeper way to his disciples and shares his heart with them in a special manner. He gives them particular tasks and responsibilities, even sending them to preach in his place.

This phase begins by Jesus calling his first disciples. The first four men he calls are two sets of brothers, Peter and Andrew, and James and John. He says to these fishermen, "Come, follow me, and I will make you fishers of men." They leave everything and follow him.

First disciples called

Jesus begins ministering in the synagogue at Capernaum, where he preaches and casts out demons (Mark 1:21ff). News about him quickly spreads all throughout Galilee as he and his disciples travel to various homes, towns and synagogues preaching, teaching, healing and casting out demons (Matt. 4:23-25). Christ is meeting people's needs, felt and real.

As they return home to Capernaum, Jesus continues to teach with his disciples at his side. As he heals the paralytic, he emphasizes the value of spiritual healing above physical healing. He says, "Which is easier to say, 'Your sins are forgiven,' or to say, 'Get up and walk'? ...the Son of Man has authority on earth to forgive sins..." (Luke 5:23-24). Jesus casts a vision for something beyond the physical realm.

Minister with the disciples

Jesus calls Matthew to join him as a disciple and Matthew responds by throwing a banquet for him, his disciples and a bunch of sinners (Mark 2:13ff). Matthew is a tax collector who comes from a different walk of life than his fishermen counterparts. His trade, however, doesn't make him any more popular among the greater public. In fact, by social standards, Jesus certainly hasn't recruited a very impressive group of men for his core team.

Evangelism

The miracles and teaching continue as Jesus models for his disciples the kind of ministry he called them to do—first alongside him and eventually without him. Amidst this busy time of ministry, Jesus regularly slips away to get alone with the Father. Even the Messiah needs time alone with his Father to refocus and reenergize for the ministry at hand. We see him equipping his disciples to reproduce what he has done in them. He teaches them and demonstrates caring for people and proclaiming the message of grace and truth. Many more people begin to respond to the claims of Jesus and his disciples.

Ministry Process

These six to nine months must have passed quickly for Jesus and his disciples, but they were very significant. Christ's choice to intentionalize time with a few is a key element of his approach to ministry. It was not in conflict with his compassion for the masses. Rather, it was in response to it. He developed disciplemakers who could make more disciplemakers as a strategy for enabling more people to encounter God and his Story. The growth of the Great Commandment values in the life of Christ and his followers led Christ to prioritize time with a few in order to expand his ministry and then mobilize them for outreach. These became the key ministry priorities for him during this phase.

Great Commission Priorities

5. Prioritizing a Few

Christ equips more than just the twelve apostles (not yet appointed) to do ministry, although the Twelve are among the larger number he equips. For those who want to go beyond Christ's initial challenge, "Follow me," he broadens his challenge to "Follow me and fish for men." Notice the nature of his challenge to his followers in calling them to minister with him.

Initially, he simply wanted people who would make themselves available for ministry (Luke 5:1-3). Next he challenges Peter's faith by telling him to put his nets in the water, even though Peter hasn't caught anything all night long. Peter did so willingly, demonstrating his faithfulness (Luke 5:4-5). As Jesus filled their nets with fish, Peter, James and John were humbled and longed to know Jesus more. Jesus wanted teachability (Luke 5:6-10a) in those with whom he would spend intentional time. Jesus used this as an opportunity to tell them that they would now join him in fishing for men and I don't sense they hesitated for even a minute. It appears that they immediately responded (Luke 5:10b-11).

As Jesus intentionalizes time with those who had been loyal believers, he begins to equip them for the work of the ministry. His idea of equipping is not a weekly meeting where he covers a curriculum in a workbook (although if he was in your context today, perhaps he would use a workbook!). Jesus' equipping is very active. He uses experiential learning and on the job training to teach his followers.

As Jesus continues to embrace and model the Great Commandment values and challenges his followers to do the same, we continue to see the presence of the vertical and horizontal patterns of growth described in the last chapter (Word, worship, community, serving). Then, as he prioritizes time with a few, he uses the same pattern to begin mobilizing them for outreach.

Priorities

1. Word
2. Worship
3. Community
4. Serving
5. Prioritizing a Few

6. Mobilizing For Outreach

Jesus mobilizes the "few" by modeling and teaching them in the process of evangelism, including cultivating, planting and reaping.

As Jesus builds intentional relationships with people and expresses love for them, we see him modeling this first priority of cultivating relationships with lost people. Jesus draws people to himself through his grace, which requires him to spend time with lost people. This is evident in events like the gathering at Peter's home when the curious community come for healing, freedom and entertainment (Mark 1:29-34). Jesus does not discourage this. Likewise, Jesus spends time with sinners when Matthew hosts a banquet at his house for Jesus and the other disciples (Luke 5:29). As a result, we see crowds from every region seeking Jesus (Matt. 4:25). All too often we skip this part of the process of evangelism. Many times, we immediately share truth with people without first breaking up the soil and earning a right to be heard.

The next phase in the process of winning lost people comes naturally to Jesus because of the way he personally embraces the priority of the Word and an understanding of who he is. As a result, Jesus demonstrates the act of planting as part of the process of evangelism. He plants seeds of truth about the reality of himself and his kingdom. It is not enough to simply spend time with lost people. The seeds of truth must be planted in the ground as it is cultivated. Jesus answers the Pharisees' questions (Luke 5:30-35; 6:1-5) and asks them questions of his own (Luke 6:6-11). He usually follows miracles by talking about the real needs of people—the ones that reach far beyond felt, physical needs.

Finally, we find Jesus reaping a life-changing harvest with lost people. As he casts vision with a sense of expectancy, he calls for a response. He challenges people to repent (Matt. 4:17; Luke 24:47) and believe (Mark 5:35-36). He forgives a man and blesses him with healing (Mark 2:1-12). He extends an intensified challenge and loses followers as a result (John 6:61-66).

Jesus spends time equipping his followers in this process of evangelism by bringing them along as he travels the land and by interacting with them about the events as they occurred. The public nature of his ministry is growing. He emphasizes both the importance of caring for one another and sharing the gospel with lost people. As noted earlier, Jesus and his team engage in aggressive evangelism in Capernaum and in the surrounding area of Galilee. Jesus recognizes that the ongoing maturity of his team of followers requires that they begin regularly reaching out to others with the gospel. The disciples had been taking in spiritual food and now they need spiritual exercise. His plan was that reaching out to lost people would become a way of life for them.

It is important to remember that evangelism did occur before this phase. The leaders had been proclaiming Christ and a natural, personal evangelism had been taking place as new disciples told their friends about Jesus. However, the importance of outreach intensifies in this phase, as well as the energy spent on equipping the team and providing contexts for them to reach out together.

True to Jesus' character, he uses the process of evangelism in many different ways and prepares his disciples to do the same. He evangelizes in one-on-one encounters, small group settings and large group gatherings. He personally evangelizes and sends out his disciples in pairs to do likewise (Mark 6:7-13). In order to do personal evangelism, Jesus and his disciples build bridges with people, often drawing from personal experiences and asking questions.

Jesus used small group settings to evangelize at times, such as when he went to Peter's and Matthew's homes (Mark 1:29-34; Luke 5:27-32). Common ground with people in the group and the use of dialogue are natural strengths of this method of evangelism. Small groups also allow multiple people to share about the reality of Christ in their lives with the lost person(s) present.

The Gospels also include many examples of Jesus' use of large groups to evangelize. He often used miracles and demonstrations of the reality of God and challenged the religious norms to communicate his message (Matt. 4:23-25). While sometimes over-used, there is a place for large group evangelism, including a presentation of the gospel, time for inter-

Priorities

1. Word

2. Worship

3. Community

4. Serving

5. Prioritizing a Few

6. Mobilizing for Outreach

action, and some sort of activity or event to bring people together in the first place.

Jesus says to his Father, "I have brought you glory on earth by completing the work you gave me to do" (John 17:4). Dann Spader, Sonlife's executive director, often asks people, "How do you explain Jesus' statement in this verse given its occurrence before the cross? What is it he has completed?" Spader makes the compelling argument that the answer lies in Jesus' statement a few verses later. "As you sent me into the world, I have sent them into the world" (John 17:18).

Jesus' mission would not have been complete apart from his death on the cross. However, his public ministry centered around calling followers and equipping them to do what he had done. His mission was the enduring mandate he gave us—to make disciples who make disciples.

CHAPTER EIGHT

Multiplying Himself
Luke 6:12 – Acts

As the fall before Jesus' spring crucifixion approaches, he intensifies his efforts to multiply himself through his disciples. People from more than six regions are pressing in on him because of his emphasis on outreach over the previous six to nine months (Mark 3:17-19). His ministry is growing and his time on earth is quickly coming to an end. So Jesus appoints some of his disciples as apostles to meet the increasing needs of the advancing kingdom.

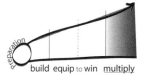

Alone with the Father

One of the times we specifically read about Jesus spending time alone with the Father is just before this appointment of the twelve apostles (Luke 6:12ff). He spends the night talking with God. The next morning, he appoints twelve from his many disciples to be close to him as apostles. They will be sent out as his messengers with delegated authority and will now be with Christ on a full-time basis.

Appoints the Twelve

Christ then breaks into the greatest sermon of all time, the Sermon on the Mount (Matthew 5-7). (Though crowds were likely listening, it seems that Jesus was targeting his newly appointed disciples. In fact, the Sermon on the Mount was a kind of "ordination sermon" for the Twelve.) Jesus condemns most of what passes as genuine religion, both then and now, by his words. He shares these compelling words not to overwhelm the disciples, but more to describe God's character and to put into perspective their character (and ours!). These powerful words have a great deal to say about life and ministry.

Sermon on the Mount

As Jesus comes down from the mountain, crowds follow him. He enters Capernaum, where a centurion asks him to come heal his servant (Luke 7:1ff). Jesus heals the servant based on the centurion's faith, and Jesus commends him to the crowd. Jesus continues to perform miracles with his disciples alongside him and he teaches creatively through parables (Matthew 13).

Jesus' intentional appointment of his apostles is an acknowledgment that he can not adequately care for the people alone, and so he entrusts some of these responsibilities to his disciples. It is important to realize that these leaders have already begun to prove themselves in ministry with Jesus. This was more than just an appointment to serve with him. They are being appointed to a position of leadership as indicated by the title "apostle," with the conferring of specific authority (Mark 3:14-15). He appoints them to spend time with him, preach and cast out demons.

Hands-on Equipping

Although the Twelve are clearly designated for future leadership roles, they are not immediately entrusted with full responsibility. In fact, at first their training looks a lot like what was given to the larger group of disciples—instruction and training on how to serve. Over time, they are released with authority and responsibility. Most of Jesus' instruction to the Twelve was accompanied by events (Matt. 26:50-56; Mark 8:14; 10:13-16; Luke 13:1), disputes (Mark 10:41-45), challenges (Matt. 17:24-27; Mark 2:18-22; 10-1-10;), observations (Mark 4:1-40; 12:41-44), questions (Mark 9:11-12, 38-41; Luke 11:1ff), and comments (Mark 13:1-37). "Almost anything could become grist to Jesus' mill" writes Robert Banks. "…Jesus relied mostly on dialogue, not presentation."[1]

After Jesus appoints and commissions his apostles, they are sent out to preach the gospel and heal the sick (Luke 9:6). He equips them with the needed skills and information to do this ministry and goes out with them (Matthew 10-11). Furthermore, they have been watching Jesus first hand for the past several months. As Jesus sends them out, he does not abandon them. They come back together, report to Jesus what happened, and they try to spend time together, away from the crowds (Luke 9:10).

Jesus stretches the apostles' faith with the feeding of the 5,000 and finds they don't yet grasp the supernatural power available to them in the Father (Matt. 14:15ff). After this, Jesus sends the disciples to the other side of the lake for their next stop while he slips away to get some time alone with the Father. In the middle of the night, the disciples row into rough waters and suddenly see a ghost walking toward them, who turns out to be Jesus. Peter, who is often criticized in this story, has faith beyond his fellow disciples because at least he gets out of the boat. Though he doubts and falls short part way through, he at least gets out of the boat and experiences Christ in ways beyond his onlooking friends. The disciples respond by saying, "Truly you are the Son of God" (Matt. 14:33b); but just a few days later, their lack of faith resurfaces when Jesus calls upon them to feed the four thousand men and their wives and children (Matt. 15:19ff).

Faith-stretching
Experiences

Jesus keeps bringing the disciples back to the same points, growing their faith bit by bit. Each time, they come with a slightly deeper level of commitment, but always with a mixture of apprehension. This is not unlike how God interacts with Israel, bringing them back to the same points, continually renewing his covenants with them. Actually, this is a lot like his pursuit of me in my struggles with faith. I rarely struggle any more questioning the foundational aspects of my faith. I know I am a wretched sinner and I know God loves me unconditionally. I am confident Jesus is the only way to have relationship with God. However, I often waiver in daily living out my faith.

For example, my faith often grows so weak when I really try to internalize Peter's words: "His divine power has given us everything we need for life and godliness" (2 Pet. 1:3a). I long to really own that in my life, but I so often doubt the truth of that statement! Or take the half million dollars we need to raise over the next three years to advance our international vision at Sonlife. Some mornings I stare at that prayer request in my journal and almost roll my eyes at the ridiculousness of it.

Jesus continues to do with me what he did with his disciples. He keeps growing my faith through new challenges and experiences.

During these last few months of Jesus' ministry, Peter, James and John get the experience of a lifetime. They must have never been the same after going up that mountain with Jesus (Luke 9:28ff). They see Moses and Elijah talking with Jesus in his glory and hear God the Father say, **Transfiguration** "This is my Son, whom I have chosen; listen to him" (Luke 9:35b). Yet shortly afterward, they join the other apostles in arguing about who is going to be the greatest. Jesus uses a child to remind them of what and whom he values.

Jesus sends out the Seventy-Two (or Seventy) to heal the sick and to preach the message of the kingdom, and they return to report (Luke 10). Many believe Jesus sent his apostles out in pairs to co-lead this larger group of workers. Regardless, Jesus continues to stretch his apostles' faith and prepares them to take his place on earth soon. Luke 12 is a **72 sent out in pairs** compelling passage mixed with both warnings and encouragements, spoken first to Jesus' core disciples while the crowds listened in the background. The opposition grows from the religious leaders, and Jesus confrontationally challenges their hypocritical leadership.

In the upper room, Jesus confers the kingdom on his apostles. They will rule and reign with Christ as shepherds under him. As he talks to them about this, he reminds them of the importance of a servant attitude (Luke 22:25). Jesus summarizes almost all of his teaching to his **Upper Room** apostles before his imminent arrest and crucifixion. He makes a number of promises to them (John 14-17). He tells them to anticipate arrest and imprisonment as God's means of multiplying the movement to people who would otherwise never be reached (Luke 21:12-13).

I won't take much time here to recount the moving events of Christ's last hours before death and the days immediately following. We've studied and preached those passages from Christ's life as much or more than any others, but with good reason. The brutal murder of Christ for and by me, the heart-wrenching separation from the Father, and Christ's miraculous resurrection are the low and high points of the Story. These elements of Christ's life mean everything to me. I deserve hell, but God has given me complete forgiveness and an eternal relationship with him. No one can ever take that from me!

Death and Resurrection

After Jesus' crucifixion and resurrection, he spends some meaningful time with the Twelve just before giving them the Great Commission. That brings us back full circle to that mountain top overlooking the Sea of Galilee, where Jesus said, "All authority in heaven and on earth has been given to me. Therefore, go and make disciples of all nations" (Matt. 28:18-19a).

As Jesus ascends to heaven and later gives believers the Holy Spirit, the disciples begin to actively multiply the ministry Jesus began. We quickly see the fruit of Jesus' ministry in the first five chapters of Acts. We read about more converts from the apostles' ministry than in all of Jesus' ministry, resulting from the foundation Christ established during his time on earth. The groundwork had been laid for multiplication. The book of Acts and the Epistles that follow describe an increasing scope of influence and movement as the Great Commission is carried out. The early church and the apostles continue the process modeled by Jesus.

Early Church

By studying Acts and Paul's writings, it becomes clear that Paul almost always took other people along on his missionary travels. He continued the collegial nature of ministry modeled by Christ. At some time or another, at least forty people linked up with Paul in this way. Paul's "roving little community of apostles was at once a training school, a miniature church, and a mutual source of support in a very difficult vocation."[2] As Paul multiplied himself through others, he was clearly the leader, yet Christ remained the pivotal person (1 Cor. 3:5-15).

Ministry Process

Just as ministry is a process, so is handing it off to those God has called to be leaders. Leadership multiplication is a process that involves identifying those followers who should be leaders, appointing and equipping them, and releasing them to lead the ministry. Failure to intentionally multiply demonstrates a ministry built around the leader rather than selflessly building the ministry around God and his Story. The embodiment of the Great Commandment values in the lives of Jesus and his disciples was used by God to continue the Great Commission priorities of the Word, worship, community and serving, as well as his prioritizing time with a few and mobilizing them for outreach. Further, God led the Son to multiply leaders.

Great Commission Priorities

7. Multiplying Leaders

Priorities

Word

Worship

Community

Serving

Prioritizing a Few

Mobilizing for Outreach

Multiplying Leaders

Jesus' night alone with the Father prior to the morning he appointed his apostles is not coincidence. He takes seriously the men who will carry on the work he began. Does Jesus decide who his apostles will be before this night of prayer? We can only speculate. We can be sure, though, that Jesus chooses those who have proven themselves as faithful workers and who are anointed by the Father to be in a leadership role. The followers not anointed as apostles should not take it as an insult. God has shaped them for other roles. But Jesus identifies those who will lead the multiplication of his ministry and then appoints them. We do our ministries and workers a disservice when we place people not proven for ministry in leadership positions. At the same time, Christ's training of the Twelve is clearly different from the way many of us were trained for ministry. Banks writes, "It was not preparation of the Twelve for mission that was uppermost in his mind, but engagement of the Twelve in mission."[3] We must equip emerging leaders by engaging them in ministry, not simply theorizing about ministry with them.

Christ's appointment is accompanied by the strong challenge of the Sermon on the Mount. Their commissioning does not entail a great deal of ceremony. It is an awakening to reality. Jesus mostly equips workers for ministry through on the job training. He teaches them as they experience ministry with him. First they watch him and then they do it with him. Next they do it on their own with his input, and then they return to report what happened and get his feedback. Jesus continues to challenge them as they spend time together. As Luke 9:57-62 illustrates, Jesus does not water down the sacrifice that comes with ministry:

> As they were walking along the road, a man said to him "I will follow you wherever you go." Jesus replied, "Foxes have holes and birds of the air have nests, but the Son of Man has no place to lay his head." He said to another man, "Follow me." But the man replied, "Lord, first let me go and bury my father." Jesus said to him, "Let the dead bury their own dead, but you go and proclaim the kingdom of God." Still another said, "I will follow you, Lord; but first let me go back and say good-by to my family." Jesus replied, "No one who puts his hand to the plow and looks back is fit for service in the kingdom of God."

As he prepares to ascend to the Father, Christ confers on the Twelve both the privilege and responsibility of leadership. As this occurs, they multiply themselves. The Epistles demonstrate disciplemaking leaders multiplying themselves for the purposes of evangelism, church planting, nurturing believers and equipping others (2 Tim. 4:1-5).

Just as people who are not proven and gifted for leadership are a disservice to themselves and others, leaders who are ill-equipped are as much of a liability, if not more. We are responsible to follow Jesus' model of faithfully equipping those he brings us to appoint as leaders. That appointment must be followed with equipping before releasing them with full responsibility.

Notes

[1]Robert Banks, *Reenvisioning Theological Education: Exploring a Missional Alternative to Current Models* (Grand Rapids: Eerdmans, 1999), 106.

[2]J. Grassi, *A World to Win: The Missionary Methods of St. Paul the Apostle* (Maryknoll, NY: Orbis, 1965), 81.

[3]Banks, 111.

Part II Conclusion

Jesus' mandate was to make disciples by seeking out the lost, identifying followers of Christ with the person and work of Christ and equipping them to minister to others. God has used the people of God, the family and his chosen leaders to accomplish his movement throughout history. Jesus modeled loving God and loving others through his life and ministry. Those values surfaced in the Great Commission priorities by building a ministry that emphasized the Word, worship, community and serving; by equipping workers to win others by prioritizing a few and mobilizing them for outreach; and by multiplying himself through his leaders, the apostles.

Part III Ministry Leadership

Your Life and

Ministry

Connecting Your Journey with the Story of God:
Disciplemaking in Diverse Contexts

Part III Overview

The Great Commandment values that characterized Christ as a person and leader, as well as the organic process he used to make disciples, are transferable to our lives and ministries. There's no question that the contexts are different and that our places in history are remarkably unlike his. He was initiating the kingdom of God and he was God in the flesh. Likewise, the early church found itself in the unique time period immediately following Christ's earthly ministry. We have the benefit of building on the many centuries of the kingdom's movement since that time. We often put the early church on a pedestal, and with good reason—given the obvious work of the Spirit and the continuation of Christ's process of making disciples. At the same time, should we not, in some ways, go beyond what was evident in those earlier years? Nearly two thousand years later in the Story, we should see strength in our ministries that not only compares with, but supersedes what existed in the early church. Regardless, the Great Commandment values of loving God and loving others and the organic process of ministry remains the same. There is a DNA of ministry that is consistent.[1]

What does Christ's example mean for our unique contexts of ministry? Remnants of the church, whether scattered or gathered, exist in every geopolitical nation of the world. How does the church continue the process of making disciples modeled by Jesus and continued by the early church? How should the church contextualize that process in diverse cultures?

As globalization overruns the world, companies like Coca-Cola® have done a masterful job of using a packaged approach to put their product into the hands of people on every continent. Coke®'s approach seems to work in most any setting. The problem, however, comes when we try to reproduce living things in the same way. All too often people attempt to advance the kingdom of God like Coke®, using a packaged approach that has worked well in one context, assuming it will work just as well in another.

Living things like rose bushes may look very different in two distinct places. If you and I both plant a rose bush near our homes, the variable

DNA (dioxyribonucleic acid) is an essential part of the human gene makeup that helps determines the physical characteristics of a person as he/she develops.

soils, insects and climates in our respective places may significantly alter how we each care for our plants. Both plants may end up looking very different, but they will both go through the same organic process. All plants grow the main stem or trunk before the branches, and grow buds before the leaves blossom—no matter what color, shape or size they are.

In the same way, local church ministry will look very different depending on the context in which it occurs. In fact, few things sadden me more than when I go to another culture, walk into a church and find all the same songs, programs, and approaches as I find at home. Sadly, evangelical missions has traditionally been one of the biggest contributors to Western colonialization. Churches around the world ought to be relevant to their respective cultures in order to redeem them.

However, there is an organic life process that must occur regardless of the context. I am pretty confident that if Jesus were to minister at my church, he would not find twelve fishermen and travel the land with them. His core group of twelve had special significance for Israel and its make-up reflects the role of males in first-century Jewish society. Regardless, I expect Jesus would follow the same overall process he used during his ministry 2,000 years ago. That same process surfaces in the diverse churches present in the Epistles, even though each church looks unique because of its context.

Sookhdeo of Guyana writes,

> The Bible, though written over a period of more than 1000 years in the context of various Middle Eastern cultures, remains relevant to every age of history, to every culture in the world, and to every situation people can enter.[2]

These final chapters require a greater deal of interactivity on the part of the reader. Use the pages that follow as tools to think through your context and the implications of Jesus' process of ministry for you there. Few if any people know your context as well as you do. The process of disciplemaking has transcended many unique contexts and time periods—but what are the implications of using this process in your ministry? By wrestling with that question, you and I have the opportunity to seriously consider the way our lives and ministries connect with the movement of God and thereby continue the Story of God.

In order to understand how to connect our lives and ministries with the greater Story, we will begin by assessing the presence of the Great Commandment in our lives. We will consider the role of the Preparation Phase in our journeys by reflecting upon our contexts. We will then look at the Great Commission priorities throughout the various phases of the process modeled by Christ. We must be faithful to live out the Great Commandment as we make disciples, and we must further structure our ministries for the appropriate Great Commission priorities. However, it is ultimately the Holy Spirit who makes the ministry happen. We cannot guarantee results simply by working on the Great Commandment values. Paul writes, "So neither he who plants, nor he who waters is anything, but only God, who makes things grow" (1 Cor. 3:7). At the same time, Jesus says, "If a man remains in me and I in him, he will bear much fruit" (John 15:5) and Paul writes, "A man reaps what he sows" (Gal. 6:7). There is clearly a correlation between how we minister and the impact that results.

> Seriously consider the way our lives and ministries connect with the movement of God and thereby continue the Story of God.

The tension lies in our measurement of that impact. I wrestle with the question, Does my faithful, strategic ministry guarantee that I will personally see the resulting harvest? If I consider men like Jeremiah, Nahum or even John the Baptist, I think I know the answer. The key lies in my remaining faithful to doing ministry like Christ, and he promises results, even if they occur after my lifetime or in a manner different than I expect.

Notes

[1]DNA (dioxyribonucleic acid) is an essential part of the human gene makeup that helps determines the physical characteristics of a person as he/she develops. Here we use the concept of DNA to describe the essential parts of ministry that determine its characteristics as it moves through the organic process of development.

[2]P. Sookhdeo, "Cultural Issues in Partnership in Mission," in *Kingdom Partnerships for Synergy in Missions*, ed. W. Taylor (Pasadena, CA: William Carey Library, 1994), 50.

CHAPTER NINE

Living the Great Commandment
Matthew 22:34 - 40

As we saw earlier, loving God and loving others were the all-consuming values of Christ's life. They are what motivated him to make disciples. These values are what permeated who he was and what he called others to be. As we embrace these values in our own lives, it will be contagious among others in our ministries. As we make them our consuming passion, God will use them to plant seeds that will result in Great Commission priorities. Our ministry priorities will flow out of who we are and what we value. The next few pages are an opportunity for us to examine the strength of each of these values in our personal lives. We must never stop giving attention to these values and we must call others to embrace them with us. As you examine each area in your life, notice the consistency of their presence throughout all the phases of ministry—preparation, building, equipping and multiplying.

Ask God to show you where you need growth in these Great Commandment values.

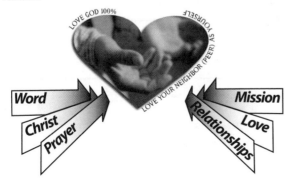

1. Prayer

We have the same resource available to us as Jesus did—the ability to connect any time, any place with the God of the universe through prayer. Like Jesus, we must make prayer a priority (Mark 1:35). Our battle is not against flesh and blood (Eph. 6:10-18); throughout God's Story we see him responding to the prayers of his people.

We must personally prioritize praying for the total needs of our ministry and for the individual members. We must challenge others to join us in this priority. Judy Foo is the youth director at Bedok Methodist Church in Singapore. She demonstrates prayerful dependence in the seriousness with which she prays for her youth and in her persistence to recruit others to do so with her. Every youth cell group has a prayer warrior who prays specifically for each member in the group. Some of the prayer warriors have shared special insights God has given them for the rest of the group. Meaningful relationships have been developed between several youth and their prayer warriors.

Here we are not talking so much about the prayer that happens corporately when your group of believers gathers. Obviously that is important, and is a natural outgrowth of prayerful dependence in your life and the personal lives of those in your ministry. But the focus here is more on the priority of prayer in your life as a disciplemaker and in the private lives of those in your group.

- What priority do you personally give prayer in your own life and for your ministry?
- Evaluate the area of prayer for your group. To what degree is prayer happening among your group members outside your meeting times?
- Who else is praying for your ministry?
- What can you do first to strengthen prayerful dependence in your ministry?

Jesus modeled a lifestyle of personal prayer in front of his disciples. They often saw him slipping away to be with the Father. He taught them how to pray (Matthew 6). Further, he pulled them aside to pray with him.

- If my prayer life was mirrored by those I want to equip, their prayer lives would be:

  ❏ sporadic   ❏ consistent   ❏ dynamic   ❏ _____

While we must be faithful to develop relationships with people and share Christ with them, it is ultimately a spiritual battle. Workers must be equipped to see the priority of prayerful dependence in ministering to others. Ministry teams must pray together as they prepare to care for their peers and share Christ with them. We must instill the value of prayer as a tangible way to care for our peers.

You might have your workers jointly develop a "Most Wanted List," the ten people you most want to see come to Christ. Who is on your *personal* "Most Wanted List"?

If anything, we see Christ intensifying his commitment to time alone with the Father as his ministry nears the point of multiplication. Identification and multiplication of leadership is a crucial step requiring fervent prayer! Further, he prays protection for his disciples as they minister in a hostile world (John 17:14-15).

It's hard for me to sit still. Just ask Linda! It drives her crazy to watch me pace around the house whenever I talk on the phone. I often find I must walk by the river near our house to best focus my dialogue with God or to use down times while driving or riding the train to talk with God. At the same time, despite the diligence it requires, there are times I need to sit in stillness and quietness and just be with God—talking to him, listening to him.

Larry Crabb writes, "In our demand that we be practical, we have nudged the Spirit aside and have gone after objectives we can reach without him."[1] May our ministries be so Spirit-dependent that people look at them and conclude, "Only God could have done that!"

2. Christ

I have been convinced for years that children growing up in North American churches are programmed to respond by answering "Jesus" to any question asked of them in church. The child may be daydreaming about the activities or snacks awaiting them and not listening to the teacher; however, most of the time, if they are called on, they can respond by saying "Jesus!!" and they will have the right answer.

Obviously Christ-centered ministry to children is a wonderful thing, as are children's perceptions of Christ. However, many times we never move beyond our immature understandings of Jesus. Many people in our ministries have wrong perceptions of who Christ is, what he's done for us and who we are in him. Many have never grown in their own understanding of Jesus. It is very difficult to yield your life to someone you do not know rightly. Proper motivation to serve and minister flows out of a growing understanding of Jesus.

This pattern is consistent with all of Scripture. Our performance comes from our understanding of God's character. In Exodus 20, the Ten Commandments are preceded by an emphasis on who God is and what he had done for his people. As Isaiah comes to know God and sees him he responds, "Here am I, send me!" (Isa. 6:8). Romans 12:1-2 urges total commitment in light of "God's mercy." Ephesians and Colossians begin with an emphasis upon what Christ has given us before shifting attention to our needed response of holiness.

- How does your cultural context view Christ? In other words, how would the average person in your neighborhood describe Jesus?
- How are you growing in your understanding of Christ? Are you more inclined to focus on what you must do for Christ or on what he has done for you?
- If your understanding of Christ were the only representation people in your ministry had of Jesus, how well would they know him?
- How do people in your ministry perceive Christ? How is their understanding of Christ furthering or hindering growth in your group?

Peter's growing understanding of Jesus is his impetus for following him. As we continually bring our groups into contact with who God is, what he's done for us and who we are in Christ, we allow the Spirit to challenge them to make him known to others. Disciples of Christ need to be gripped with who Christ is to them personally so that they cannot help but share him with the people in their world.

We should regularly give people opportunities to declare their commitment to following Christ. Workers need to be equipped to encourage one another in Christlikeness throughout the week.

- The first word I want my equipped believers to use to describe Christ is _____.

We must continually remind our workers that Jesus is the greatest need of their lost friends. We must challenge them to move beyond simply trying to be a sounding board for peers and help them truly bring Jesus into their friendships.

Christ continually deepened his apostles' understanding of him and his program as he prepared to send them out. As we begin to grasp that Christ, God himself, released leaders to multiply his ministry, surely we will see our need to do the same. Long before we even get to the point where we can multiply leaders, we need to have multiplication in view. It is the central ingredient of Christ's approach to ministry.

How do we communicate a right understanding of Christ? Our personal understanding of Jesus is a key ingredient in shaping our group's understanding of Jesus. Our character speaks more powerfully than our words. We cannot take people where we have not been ourselves. Our instruction and our nonverbal lifestyle and actions must emphasize not what we are to do for God but instead, who God is, what he has done for us and who we are in Christ.

3. Word

One of my greatest fears is boring people with the Bible. The Bible is so much more than a how-to manual for life or a book of propositional truths. The Bible is far more dynamic than that. It is straight from the God of the universe. God's Word consistently reveals the unfolding of who God is and humanity's relationship to him.

As a result, the Word interprets us more than we interpret it. We are not lord over the text; it is lord over us. We must engage in the Story of God through his Word. We must beware of worshiping the Word and never getting to the Hero to whom all of Scripture points. *Jesus* is the point of the Story.

- How are you doing personally with the discipline of reading, studying, memorizing and meditating on the Word of God?
- Do you find yourself engaging with the Story of God as you read the Word, or is it merely an academic or ritualistic practice?
- How well do people in your ministry know the Word?

Jesus saw Scripture as the basis for his disciples' freedom. As it transformed their lives, Scripture was their lifeline for how to minister to others. Jesus taught his disciples skills for ministry (Mark 6:6-12; John 13:12-17).

We must train workers to not only be in the Word, but also to use it as the backbone for ministry to others. We need to help them work on how to meaningfully introduce the Word of God into any conversation.

- People in our ministry see Scripture as:

  ❐ narrow   ❐ irrelevant   ❐ road map   ❐ _____

Christ used Scripture to bring people to their points of need (i.e. rich young ruler). We must assist those God brings us to use the Word as a tool for ministry. They must continually use the Word as a personal lifeline as well as learn how to use it to minister to others. The Word must be presented as God's Story while inviting people to see their journey as part of that story.

- To what degree are your workers equipped to use the Word in ministering to others?

Christ quoted Isaiah 35:4-6 in response to John the Baptist's questions about his ministry. Our work with our leaders must be grounded in the Word. We must be carefully listening to God as we multiply ourselves and the ministries he gives us. New leaders must be equipped to study, teach and live the Word. They must learn how to teach others to do the same.

I personally study the passages of Scripture I plan to teach six months to a year before I actually teach them. This makes my teaching of those passages far enough away so that I am less inclined to circumvent applying the Scripture to my own life, and focusing entirely on how to apply it to others. At the same time, it keeps my teaching close enough to my personal study of that passage and its penetration of my own life so that my teaching flows from my heart.

God's Word has supernatural power to change lives—ours and those to whom we minister (Heb. 4:12; John 8:31-32); and it gives us the clearest revelation of who God is, what he's done for us and who we are in Christ. The priority of the Word is foundational to all we are and do in life and ministry.

4. Relationships

Relationships are the essential context for disciplemaking. I struggle with how to make them both intentional and informal. I must be proactive in pursuing relationships with people, yet relationships are not one more thing I can or should program and control.

There have been adults and students all throughout my ministry experience to whom I am drawn and visa versa. We have an affinity that comes easily and it does not take much effort to intentionalize time together. The reverse is also true. I have neglected time with many people in my ministry contexts because they drained me. While Christ prioritized time with his disciples, I never see him avoiding or neglecting people. He always had time for the outcast. Further, he used his time with the disciples to foster, through them, even more relationships.

- What are the benefits of building relationships with people in their everyday world?

Howard Hendricks writes,

> You can impress people at a distance, you can only impact them up close. The general principle is: The closer the personal relationship, the greater the potential for impact. [2]

We do not need to try to become like everyone in our ministries, but others do need to see that we love, understand and accept them. Going where they are allows us to impart "not only the gospel of God but our lives as well" (1 Thess. 2:8).

- Name the top five sermons which have influenced you.
- Name the top five people who have influenced you.
- Which list was easier to make? If you're like most people, the latter is much easier. Why? Because "more is caught than taught."
- How well are you building relationships with people outside the formal church setting?
- What are practical ways you can initiate building relationships with people in your ministry?
- What are the barriers to building these relationships? How can you overcome these barriers?
- Who else can or does join you in building intentional relationships with people?

As we develop relationships with people in our ministry outside the church, we will gain a better understanding of whether they are ready for something more than just receiving ministry. We must share life with them, and model and challenge them to be available, faithful, teachable and responsive.

- My time devoted to being with those I need to equip is:
  ❑ nonexistent   ❑ random   ❑ prioritized   ❑ _____

Jesus intentionalized personal visits like the one he made to Zacchaeus' home (Luke 19:1-10). As we begin to see God surface workers to join us in ministry, we must begin training them to intentionalize relationships. We must first and foremost instill in them the priority that ministry means serving people.

Eventually, we will challenge our workers to intentionalize relationships with people and develop a strategy to share Christ with them.

• Do believers in your ministry have lost friends?

Christ did not abandon his leaders when he released them. As the leader spends time with the workers God has surfaced, he/she must be alert to who God has gifted and called to leadership. The leader must instill in potential leaders the ongoing importance of intentional relationships. They need to be equipped to teach others to intentionalize relationships.

For a few years, I worked for a Christian university and spent a great deal of time as an itinerant speaker to youth. One day, a student from a church where I had pastored called and asked me what I was doing now. As I began to explain it to him, he said, "Well, no offense Dave, but in the years you were our pastor, I only remember a couple of things you ever said when you were preaching. What I remember most about you were all the times we spent together at your apartment, the trips we took together and the times when you were driving down the road and suddenly asked our forgiveness for your bad attitude about something. So what makes you think these kids you are talking to are really remembering anything you are saying when you come in and out for an hour or two or even for a weekend retreat?" Wow!

I don't mean to dismiss God's use of preaching to change lives, but far more often we see Jesus using the power of relationships. Our preaching is strengthened by a growing personal relationship with others. Ninety percent of discipling is relationships—so the question is not *whether* building relationships should be part of discipling, but *how* to effectively build relationships with people in our ministries.

5. Love

How do we make 1 John 3:16 ("…Christ laid down his life for us. And we ought to lay down our lives for our brothers.") more than a fairy tale in our families, ministries and other relationships? We know that our lives and ministries should be known first and foremost for the love experienced and expressed there, yet so often that is easier said than done. We cannot *not* communicate. Do you really love those God has called you to shepherd? Use this section to spend some time evaluating your love for the people in your ministry.

- Evaluate your love for the members of your group. Who is most difficult to love? Why?
- Are you communicating your love to your group?
- Do people feel loved in your group? What areas need improvement?

Jesus modeled loving the unlovely. As he made love a non-negotiable approach to ministry, he was demonstrating to his disciples the kind of ministry he would call them to have.

Jesus trains his disciples, both formally and informally, in the importance of cultivating friendships that allow for influence (John 1:39). His method was to draw people by love, not by force. He wanted to train them to do the same.

As he trained them, he built them into a team (John 13:34-35). As they grew in their love for one another, they more effectively ministered together.

- When I express love to those I want to equip, I:
  ❏ manipulate   ❏ empower   ❏ encourage   ❏ _____

Training our workers must include instilling the core value of love in all that we do as we minister to one another and to others outside our group. Workers must understand the importance of love at the core of all the ministry we do. We must pursue peers with no strings attached. Love must continue unconditionally, regardless of the response or outcome. We must, like Christ, become a "friend of sinners" (Luke 7:34).

Christ continued to lead by grace rather than by force, and he challenged his disciples to make love their motive for obedience and ministry (John 15:9-13). They needed to shepherd others in expressing love to one another. Christ should be our example as we challenge others to lead with us.

It is not enough to know that you love the people in your ministry and assume they know it as well. Too many marriages grow stale because husbands and wives forego creative ways to express their love for one anther. My ministry with Sonlife requires that I travel a great deal, and often before a trip I will feel like the most loving thing I can do for Linda is to tidy up the house and finish all the odd jobs left undone. While she wants to be grateful, she usually tells me she would rather spend time with me, talking and enjoying one another's company. While I might think my acts of service are expressing love for her, she in fact sees them as a way to avoid her.

People in our ministries express and experience love in different ways, too. We must help our group members grow in this Great Commandment value by creating situations where love can be expressed.

- Evaluate the level of love expressed in your group. "And let us consider how we may spur one another on toward love and good deeds" (Heb. 10:24).

6. Mission

Jesus sees potential in people and calls them to live up to it (John 1:42, 47). He stretches their vision for what God wants to do and talks about the future with a great sense of faith (John 1:50-51; 4:35-38). He consistently points his followers to the power of God (John 14:12-14).

Our discernment of God's vision and our expectation for what God is going to do will directly affect the amount people in our ministry learn, their level of commitment to the ministry and their willingness to engage others in what the ministry is about.

I used to feel burdened by every good ministry idea someone shared with me. Somehow I felt obligated to add it to the many things our ministry was already doing. As I began to more clearly discern God's mission for the ministries I led, I was freed to pursue only those ideas that would most effectively accomplish our vision in our context.

- Draw a picture of your vision for your group. What are you praying will be true of your group over the next few years?

- How does the average person in your group perceive it? Draw a picture of how they would describe your group.

Jesus observes attitudes and behaviors contrary to the mission he had come to fulfill. In response, he challenges his disciples to follow him in his character and priorities (John 6). The heart of Jesus' mission was to equip others to lovingly reach and nurture their peers.

Part of training others in the work of the ministry involves helping them catch a vision for being fully-trained disciples who are equipped to reach and care for their peers.

- Agree/Disagree: I have a God-dependent confidence that we are going to see our ministry mature through more members reproducing their lives in the lives of others. Explain your response.

As believers express a desire to minister to others, we start by giving them a vision of caring for people within the group and then helping them to see the importance of sharing Christ out of a relationship of love. We must give them a vision of being called to make disciples of people God brings their way. Our personal priority of this will be the first step in instilling this value in our workers.

Workers must be challenged to realign their priorities to allow for time to share Christ with lost friends. They must catch the vision to be a reproducing believer and must minister to people with a sense of urgency and expectancy.

As we begin to intentionalize relationships with a few in order to equip them to do ministry, we begin by looking for those we should equip. Though we will continue to emphasize the Great Commandment values throughout the entire ministry, we must begin to think about how to reproduce these values in the lives of a few. Our ability to multiply these values in the lives of those we equip will be directly related to the degree to which we emphasize them personally.

Peter is assured he has something to offer others if he truly loves Christ (John 21:15-19). We limit our vision of what God can do in and through us if we fail to release others as leaders. The real impact of Christ's ministry occurred after he ascended to heaven. We must multiply leaders who multiply leaders.

Summary

I love to study and teach the Word, and clarify the mission. The ministries God has allowed me to lead have been historically strong in those areas because I made sure those areas happened. I am energized by those things. Other areas however, have often been weaker in my ministries. More often than I care to admit, God has had to use people and circumstances to remind me of the importance of the other vital values of a Great Commandment foundation. God has consistently surrounded me with people who remind me to stop all my great strategizing and take time to pray. I must admit that at times, when I am in the midst of passionately laying out where we need to head and working through the process, I am frustrated by the interruption from these people. But I know that it is a much-needed interruption. I am so thankful for the strength God has brought my ministry through people who insist on having us spend meaningful time together praying. I could use similar examples from other values, such as developing a loving group, intentionalizing relationships and worship. I have varying spurts of enthusiasm for each of these at different times, but I have learned the strength of pulling a diverse team of workers and leaders around me so that we consistently embrace and exercise all the values of the Great Commandment.

- What two of the 6 Great Commandment values need your attention first?

  ❒ Prayer   ❒ Christ   ❒ Word
  ❒ Relationships   ❒ Love   ❒ Mission

- List the first area you checked _____

- What are you going to do in the *next week* to work on this value?

- What do you need to do in the next 6 weeks to work on this value?

- List the second area you checked _____

- What are you going to do in the *next week* to work on this value?

- What do you need to do in the *next 6 weeks* to work on this value?

The Great Commandment values are the foundation for doing ministry like Jesus. They are the seeds we place in the soil in order to grow Great Commission priorities. Ultimately, the Holy Spirit causes the resulting growth, but we are responsible to embrace and live out these values.

Notes

[1]Larry Crabb, *The Safest Place on Earth: Where People Connect and are Forever Changed* (Nashville: Word, 1999), 126.

[2]Howard Hendricks, *Leadership Journal* (Summer 1980).

CHAPTER TEN

Understanding Your Context

Our context shapes who we are and how we think. It is the lens by which we interpret life and the framework from which we approach Scripture. Our context shapes how we make disciples. For example, in many places around the world, the church has been most effective at reaching youth by developing a specific ministry for youth as a segment of the church. This often includes young people from the age of twelve or thirteen until they are married. Other contexts have very specific breakdowns even within the adolescent years where targeted ministries are developed for 12-13-year-olds, others for 14-15-year-olds, and so on. In some Eastern cultures, ministry to youth is done most effectively by *not* developing a separate youth group per se. Instead, reaching them as part of the family unit is far more effective.

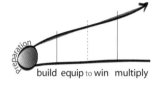

In order for you to understand and most effectively fulfill God's vision for your ministry in your context, you must take time to carefully think through your context and your Preparation Phase. You do yourself, your ministry and most importantly, God's kingdom a great disservice when you uncritically replicate ministry models from another context to yours.

In a manner similar to Jesus, Saint Patrick of England mobilized a movement of disciplemaking in Ireland by giving careful attention to the context. Missiologist George Hunter writes,

> The fact that Patrick understood the people and their language, their issues, and their ways, serves as the most strategically significant single insight that was to drive the wider expansion of

the Celtic Christianity, and stands as perhaps our greatest single learning from this movement. There is no shortcut to understanding the people.[1]

There are three important dimensions to the contexts in which we find ourselves—personal, cultural and ministry. Some would argue that it is impossible to separate our contexts into these three dimensions. Admittedly, the distinction is a fabrication, but it is one I am willing to make for the purpose of deepened analysis. I would concur that one's personal context is directly shaped by one's cultural context and that cultural context is a collaboration of personal and ministry contexts. All three contexts are symbiotically related and are impossible to separate in real life.[2] At the same time, there is value in considering the varying roles each of these contexts bring to our implementation of Christ's process of ministry.

Personal Context

Your personal context is the unique personality, giftedness and set of experiences you bring to your ministry. Just as Christ's years of preparation influenced his ministry, so your journey through life with God will influence the way you approach ministry. Your childhood and adolescence, conversion, spiritual journey, experiences with the church, roles in ministry, family, job situation, abilities, spiritual gifts and much more are all part of your personal context. Use the following questions to help you reflect on some of these areas.

- What role has church played in your journey as a disciple?
- What role has family played in your journey as a disciple?
- Draw a picture portraying your current season in life.
- Your age greatly influences your role in family ministry. For example, a 23-year-old youth leader may have more in common with youth than with the parents of youth. How does your current age influence your role in your ministry?
- In what areas of ministry does the body of Christ affirm you most? Where do you sense God's gifting in your life?
- What are some of the abilities or skills God has given you?

- What are your passions? What energizes and motivates you?
- Draw a timeline that briefly describes your spiritual journey. As you do so, think about some of the spiritual markers God has used in your life. What experiences, good or bad, have played a significant role in shaping you?

Spend some time thanking God for the unique way he has shaped you to be part of his Story. Draw upon him to turn even the seemingly negative things about your personal context into positive ways to make disciples.

Sonlife's advanced training explores the personal context much more thoroughly. Check availability of one of these seminars in your vicinity by visiting our web site: www.sonlife.com.

sonlife.com

Cultural Context

Your cultural context is the socio-cultural setting where you minister. Perhaps this is your own culture or maybe you are a foreigner in this culture. Regardless, it's important to step back and look at how the cultural context should influence the way you make disciples. Because of our common bond as Christians, adhering to cultural norms should not be the decisive response to dealing with your context. There will be times when we must transcend our cultural contexts to redeem them. However, we must carefully look at how to most effectively make disciples in light of the cultural dynamics where we minister.

Culture comes from a Latin word meaning "tilling of the soil." Most Western languages understand it to mean "civilization" or "refinement of the mind" referring especially to forms of education, art and literature. Clifford Geertz calls culture the webs of significance humanity has spun for itself.[3]

Culture represents a group's shared way of perceiving, judging and organizing ideas, situations and events as encountered in daily life. It encompasses the rules or guidelines used by people who share a common history or geographical setting to mediate their interaction with their environment. Culture might involve adhering to a specific religious orientation and use of certain language or style of communication. It may also encompass preferences for expressive methods of representing their perceptions of the world (i.e. art, music, dance). According to Geert Hofstede, culture is the "collective programming of the mind which distinguishes the members of one group or category of people from another."[4] Culture is less what people do and more the ideas they have about what they do and the materials used to do so.[5]

Perceptual development differs within various ethno-cultural groups. It is therefore erroneous in the disciplemaking process to assume that all people perceive an event, idea or object in the same way."[6] In other words, my understanding of God the Father may be notably different from yours because of our personal and cultural experiences with the role of fathers. Consequently, culture both enables and constrains one's understanding of God's Story. The disciplemaker's sensitivity to the role of culture in the way people know God and make him known to others is vitally important.

The challenges are compounded when working with a culture different than one's own. We live in a world where the dominant forces in the West are perpetuating a uniform, global culture. These forces are continually positioning themselves to increase their power and to exclude those without it. Cross-cultural disciplemakers must be careful not to repeat this pattern of forcing our own culture into others.

The cross-cultural disciplemaker must be very cautious of power issues. Rather than using an atomistic, banking approach to ministry where we view ourselves as making deposits into the recipients of our ministry, we must empower indigenous leaders to develop their own Christlike ministries. The colonial pursuits from the West would have failed without having divided the subjects in order to more effectively preserve the state of oppression. It depended upon "blinding" the oppressed.[7] Christlike disciplemaking does not invade a culture nor impose a model.

In contrast to the sadness I experience when I walk into a non-North American church that sings all the same songs and replicates all the same programs I experience in my North American church, my heart is full of joy when I experience churches like some of those among the

Akha believers in Thailand. As you walk into many Akha churches, you find all the generations together. Everyone joins in chanting, singing and dancing to words and melodies they have created themselves, accompanied by tribal instruments. They move around the area where they gather for church with great excitement as they talk about what God has done in their lives this past week; and having watched each other closely all week long, they hold one another accountable for making wrongs right with each other and with God. The teaching of the Word is interwoven all throughout the gathering of believers in a folklorish style. People share crops and livestock with one another and weep and rejoice together. Members, young and old together, are commissioned to travel to other Akha villages to make disciples.

In fact, I have been so moved by experiences like these, I have sometimes been inclined to replicate what I saw in my ministry at home. But then I am reminded that this works so well because it is a contextually appropriate way of carrying out Christ's process of ministry among Akha people.

Use the following to guide your reflection on the way your cultural context should shape the way you make disciples.

- How is church viewed by people in your culture?
- Is there a predominant religion?
- If so, how does the religion influence the worldview of your culture?
- What role does family play in your culture?
- How does family influence your ministry?
- Who holds the most power in your culture? What group of people?
- How do authority figures relate to people under their authority?
- Is leadership something to which people aspire or avoid?
- Do you think your culture places greater value on individuals or groups?
- Compare the roles of men and women in your culture. Are they clearly defined?
- How tolerant is your culture to change? Is change typically sought or avoided?
- What's the history of the Christian church in your culture? Missions?

Since youth represent a powerful resource for disciplemaking, we should all give careful thought to how we might tap into youth to fuel a movement of multiplication. Use the following questions to generate your thinking about youth in your cultural context:

- Who are their heroes?
- Do they have free time? If so, how do they use it?
- Describe how they are viewed by society at large.
- Describe the average young person's relationship with his/her parents.
- Of what does their educational system consist?
- What are their fears?
- What drives them?
- What level of interaction do youth have with adults?

Thank God for the culture where he has placed you to minister. Ask him to use you as his agent to redeem this culture—both the people and all they represent.

Ministry Context

Finally, your ministry context will significantly influence how you will go about making disciples. Our ministries are organizations with a socialization that has occurred through their history. This affects the way the disciplemaking process unfolds.

For example, some of us minister in churches where the predominant age group is younger while others minister where most of the church members are older. Still others of us are part of very intergenerational churches. Choirs are highly valued in some churches, while other congregations consider them totally unnecessary.

Your ministry has existing programs and structures with which you must work, while others may have different programs and structures. Again, there will be times when we must transcend our ministry contexts and challenge people beyond existing programs and thinking, but we must choose those areas carefully. The values of your church, its history, its leadership structure and much more should all be taken into consideration as you develop your philosophy of ministry.

- Is there a predominant age group leading your church? If so, which?
- How old is your church?
- What is your overall church structure? Who leads the church? How do they end up in leadership?
- How many people attend weekly church services?
- Is your church growing? If so, is the growth mostly a result of transfer (Christians from other churches), biological (baby Christians) or conversion (people coming to Christ)?
- What is your church's greatest strength?
- What is your church's greatest weakness?
- What role do youth play in your church?
- How do most church members view youth?
- Is there a youth group/fellowship in your church?
- If so, when do they meet? Where? What happens?
- Who is included in "youth group" (i.e. what ages, are most Christians or non-Christians)?
- What animal best depicts your church as it is today? Why?

Ask God to give you his heart for the ministry of which you are a part. Pray for the wisdom to leverage the strengths of this ministry while leading it through the weaknesses. Don't make the mistake of trying to replicate others' successful programs without giving careful thought to the implications of your unique ministry context.

Summary

The "one-size-fits-all" approach to making disciples is more than problematic. How do we follow Christ's process of making disciples without de-culturating people? How do we move disciples into new conscious choices without stripping them of their identity?

We must become experts in understanding our contexts. God did and continues to today. Even though he was the Creator of humanity and earth, he came to earth through his Son to be one of us. No one can say he doesn't know what we're going through! The more we understand our contexts, the more we will be able to effectively join God in making disciples. At the same time, as referenced previously, we must not allow our contexts to paralyze us. Our first priority is to the mission: to make disciples. How can we most effectively do so in our contexts? That's the key question. When our context prevents us from doing what we must do, we must become Spirit-dependent to transcend it.

P. Sookhdeo says it well:

> While recognizing the importance of culture in form and communication, it can no longer be the altar at which we worship, the interpreter of all we do. We need to rediscover biblical values which we all share, which transcend culture, which affirm culture, and which judge culture. We need to rediscover our biblical identity as the children of God over against our cultural affinities. We need to rediscover our common calling, that is, the evangelization of the whole world, as opposed to self-imposed cultural limits.[8]

We must plant and lead churches and ministries so indigenous that the full flavor and approach to disciplemaking emerges from the context while still embodying the counter-cultural values and priorities of the Great Commission.

Notes

[1]George G. Hunter, *The Celtic Way of Evangelism: How Christianity Can Reach the West...Again* (Nashville: Abingdon, 2000), 19-20.

[2]Jonathan H. Turner, *A Theory of Social Interaction* (Stanford: Stanford University Press, 1988).

[3]Clifford Geertz, *An Interpretation of Cultures* (New York: Basic Books, 1973).

[4]Geert Hofstede, *Cultures and Organizations: Software of the Mind* (New York: McGraw Hill, 1997), 5.

[5]Allan Johnson, *The Blackwell Dictionary of Sociology: A User's Guide to Sociological Language* (Malden, Mass.: Blackwell, 1995).

[6]B.J. Shade, "The Influence of Perceptual Development on Cognitive Style: Cross-Ethnic Comparisons," in *Early Childhood Development and Care* (1989).

[7]Paulo Freire, *Pedagogy of the Oppressed* (New York: Continuum, 1997).

[8]P. Sookhdeo, "Cultural Issues in Partnership in Mission," in *Kingdom Partnerships for Synergy in Missions*, ed. W. Taylor (Pasadena, CA: William Carey Library, 1994), 50.

CHAPTER NINE

Building Ministry in Your Context

Now that we've looked at the Great Commandment values that must permeate our lives as disciplemakers and the nature of our contexts, let's shift attention to the Great Commission priorities. Christ uses the Great Commandment values to yield these Great Commission priorities. This is more than a collection of principles for effective ministry; it is the DNA of ministry demonstrated in Christ's ministry context as well as in the context of the early church. This same DNA should flow through your ministry, but with the uniqueness of your own context.

Consider the implications of the way Christ began his public ministry. You may want to go back and peruse what Christ intentionally prioritized as he built his ministry (chapter 6). What follows is intended to stimulate thought about how to minister as Christ would minister in our unique contexts. It is a question with which we must continue to wrestle as we minister in the kingdom. Think about the Great Commandment values as lived out in the building phase of ministry and the Great Commission priorities that resulted.

What resulted from Christ's prioritization of the Great Commandment as the foundation for life and ministry? These values of loving God and others are the ingredients he put into the soil; they are what he personally lived and they are the values he called his followers to embrace. As he built his ministry, he established ministry patterns which resulted above the soil from Great Commandment living. These are the

Great Commission priorities we must emphasize when we gather believers together. These are uniquely created for followers of Christ.

Among Jesus' followers and later in the New Testament church, believers gathered around the priorities of the Word, worship, community and serving. All four may not have been present at every gathering, but they were all regular practices among the believers assembling together. Think of these four priorities as the cylinders of a four-cylinder engine. I'm not an expert when it comes to cars, but I know that a car can run for a time without all its cylinders. It won't run as effectively, though, and eventually it will die altogether. We must evaluate our ministry programs that help believers grow and analyze the balance of all four of these priorities.

> We must evaluate our ministry programs that help believers grow and analyze the balance of all four of these priorities.

Brazil is one of the countries where I have ministered often. For several years, Brazil has received more missionaries than any other country in the world. As a result, there is every variety of church throughout the country, each with its own strengths and weaknesses. In attending many Brazilian churches, I have observed several ministries running strong on one cylinder of the engine while the other cylinders sputter or appear completely dead. Some of the churches have great teaching from the Word, but the singing is weak and people have little interest in one another. In other churches, the worship time is incredible but the teaching from the Word lacks depth and people have little opportunity to serve one another. In others, Sunday morning feels like one big party, but the time in the Word is short and little time is made for the church to corporately respond to God. A healthy ministry is one where all four cylinders of the engine (Word, worship, community, serving) are running simultaneously. I suspect that what I have observed in Brazil is true in some churches in most every country and I know it's true in North America. I should say I have also observed some incredibly healthy churches in Brazil that have taught me volumes about giving attention to all four of these areas. All four are not necessarily present at every gathering of believers every time they meet, but over a short period of time, all four regularly surface and are given primary attention.

Great Commission Priorities

Remember that only the Holy Spirit ultimately causes growth. However, as we faithfully embrace and live out the Great Commandment values, we will structure our ministries around these vertical (with God) and horizontal (with others) priorities of Great Commission ministry.

1. Word

As you may recall, this priority refers to encountering the living Word of God and allowing the Spirit to mold us. Clearly this is a natural outgrowth of the Great Commandment value of God's Word in our lives as shepherds and in the lives of our sheep. There is a time, however, for communicating the Word to the group collectively—encouraging personal Bible study is not enough.

Priorities

1. Word

2. Worship

3. Community

4. Serving

5. Prioritizing a Few

6. Mobilizing for Outreach

7. Multiplying Leaders

Effective communication of God's Word depends less on communication ability and more on:

1. Developing strong habits of personal Bible study

   Read the Bible as a Story and see how the passage you are studying fits in with the broader Story. Look for the original intent of the passage. What does it tell you about God? About yourself? How will you respond to what you understand?

2. Allowing teaching to flow from personal study

3. Integrating truth and life in your teaching. A helpful outline for making your teaching connect with believers' lives is Hook, Book, Look, Took[1]:

   Hook: How will this lesson be relevant to my class? Why should they listen? How can I get them interested in this lesson?

   Book: What does the Bible say ? What was the original intent? Are students in the Word? How will I get them to explore the Word? Am I lecturing again?

   Look: What are the implications of this passage? How does this passage help us understand who God is and what he has done for us?

   Took: How will I challenge people to personally respond? How will I ask the Spirit to work in lives?

4. Common Mistakes in Handling God's Word:

- Talking a lot about the Bible without actually studying the Bible.
- Overuse of favorite subjects.
- Lack of creativity in teaching methods.
- Wandering through a random collection of verses or ideas.
- Being guided by curriculum rather than using it as a tool to help you.
- Failing to see the overall Story of the Bible as you study and teach it.
- Failing to acknowledge the baggage your context brings to your understanding and teaching of the Word.
- Worshiping the Word in itself rather than using it as a means to the real end—Jesus!
- Discounting people's interest in the Word.
- Failure to see God's Word for what it is first and foremost—the unfolding of who God is and accounts of how humanity interacts with him.

Ask yourself:

- Are people in your ministry growing in their ability to relate the Word to their lives?
- When your ministry gathers, do people interact with the Scriptures and with each other?

A few years ago, I became frustrated when I met with a small group in our youth ministry. No one came prepared. I challenged them with the importance of studying the passage before our weekly meeting, having allowed the passage to penetrate their own lives. Some of the more aggressive members spoke up. "Dave, try to see how impossible this feels to us! On Sunday mornings, we go to youth group time and you teach us from one topic. Then we go to Sunday morning worship and Pastor Rudd teaches us something else. Then we come back to church Sunday evening and hear another message. Several of us are trying to do personal devotions every day and some of us are involved in Bible studies at school. A few of us are on the ministry team, where you have us doing additional work, and then there's this Bible study. Many of our families do family devotions. Those of us who attend Christian school have Bible class every day, chapel regularly, devotions before sports practices and on it goes. And you wonder why we aren't prepared?!"

I was speechless. I knew they had made a valid point. We had made it nearly impossible for them to dig deeply into the Word. That challenged us to communicate the Word differently. Our congregation was beginning to study the book of James. In response, we decided to make James our sole focus as a youth ministry for the next year. I wrote a daily journal that our youth used throughout the week to study the passage of Scripture that would be taught the following Sunday. We would hear a message about the passage with the whole congregation, and then talk about age-appropriate applications in youth group. In small groups, we shared the personal implications of the passage for us. On our weekend retreats and other activities, James and its many topics became the common thread. I learned the hard way that communicating the Word is more than simply preparing a thirty-minute lesson. I need to help the believers in my ministry use the Word as their lifeline to God.

Don't forget the importance of Spirit-dependence through prayer and your attitude as you prepare and teach. Ultimately, the Spirit will bring about the right application!

Disciplemaking Around the World

 **Australia:** St. Martin's Church in Australia, targeting Irish immigrants, features clear and relevant teaching of the Word during services. The Word is communicated in a way that faces daily issues as well as the ultimate issues in life. Teaching features storytelling because of the way that Irish souls are deeply engaged by stories.[2]

 **Chicago:** Each Sunday when I attend my church (Christ Community Church in St. Charles, Illinois), I receive not only a sermon outline allowing me to take notes, but also a couple of pages of study questions for my own follow-up. Rather than limit the teaching of the passage of the week to the thirty-minute Sunday sermon, we are encouraged to do the follow-up study in some form—personal devotions, family devotions, accountability partners, cell groups, etc.

Gabon: On the Western Coast of Africa, Gabonese youth workers take their young people through TEE (Theological Education by Extension) courses. While the youth workers were initially told the material would be too intense and deep for the youth in their ministries, the youth proved otherwise. The youth meet in one another's homes mid-week to share the few copies of the studies that exist and prepare for their weekly cell group meetings. They look forward to getting together to learn from God as a group.

Indonesia: Because of the sparse number of people in churches to work with youth in Indonesia, many churches share a youth worker—even if they are located several hours apart. The youth take turns traveling to one another's locations so they can study the Word together. Several travel by foot for many hours on a regular basis and then spend the night with their peers in another village just for this reason. Because of the strong commitment that is demanded, the time these youth share together is deep and powerful.

How could you creatively communicate the Word in your context?

Northern Ireland: One of our ministry partners has strongly encouraged Scripture memorization in the cell groups of her ministry. Everyone memorizes at least one verse in their group each week, and they hold one another accountable for it. Youth are also encouraged to express that verse in a creative way. Some write poems or songs reflecting the meaning of the verse. Others paint pictures, create videos or write stories. The verses become much more than syllables locked away in their minds—they transform one another's lives.

Singapore: Youth often lead large group Bible studies in some Singaporean youth ministries. Drama is often used to help youth interact with the Word instead of simply talking about it. Sometimes the drama is prepared ahead of time, but other times the youth are broken into groups and randomly assigned a passage of Scripture to act out. Sometimes everyone acts out the same passage and other times each person has a unique one. After fifteen minutes to study the passage and develop an idea, youth act out their passages for each other. Groups finish by debriefing within their drama groups or with the whole group to talk about the application of the passage.

Action Plan for the Word in Your Ministry
- What are the highs and lows of this priority in your ministry?
- What ideas do you have for strengthening this priority?
- What needs to happen first?

---

2. Worship

Worship regards and adores God by glorifying him with our thoughts and actions. Worship without the nurturing of the Word is an incomplete growth experience (just as teaching the Word without worship is incomplete). Worship allows us to respond to God for all he is and does.

Priorities

1. Word

2. Worship

3. Community

4. Serving

5. Prioritizing a Few

6. Mobilizing for Outreach

7. Multiplying Leaders

- What happens at your regular gathering that directs attention upward toward God?
- Can people of diverse ages and backgrounds freely express their adoration to God at your growth times?
- Are there outlets for public worship beyond music? If so, what?
- How else can you foster public worship as a group?

Throughout my years in ministry, extended times together have often been some of the most meaningful opportunities to corporately respond to God. It's no accident that the priorities for growth fuel one another. As we build community, dig into the Word and serve God and others together, our response to God in worship becomes more meaningful. I have also found that many of our best times of responding to God happened when we didn't expect it. Sometimes after a great rehearsal, when all the instruments were perfectly tuned and the sound and lights were running well, our worship time has been weak. Other times, when sitting stranded on the side of the road, we have spontaneously begun talking aloud to God, singing, sitting quietly and reading Scripture together.

We must regularly create opportunities for believers to collectively respond to God. We must also be sensitive to times when the Spirit wants us to lead our groups in corporate worship, even if it isn't planned.

Disciplemaking Around the World

Australia: St. Martin's church in Melbourne is known for its spontaneity and openness in worship. Services are planned but also leave room for redemptive moments that are unprogrammed. They encourage the full expression of Christian imagination, featuring indigenous art with Christian themes (much is postmodern). Wall hangings by church members fill the sanctuary.[3]

England: Revelation Church in southern England works hard to discover ways to worship through visual symbols and creative arts. Sometimes during services, artists are encouraged to draw what they feel as the body worships together. Sometimes sculptors and potters work on the side during the meeting. The art often speaks for itself, while other times artists are encouraged to interpret their portrayal of worship.[4]

India: Some of my richest times of worship in recent days have been with our partnering ministries in India. As the churches in India undergo intensified persecution, their corporate times of worship also seem to intensify. Several churches I have visited allow time in their services for church members to spontaneously come forward and sing a song reflecting their hearts' desire to worship God. Before and after the song, Scripture is usually read and testimonies are shared about how God has superseded in one's life amid spiritual persecution during the week.

Kenya: Many European-driven churches in Africa have floundered because of their failure to engage Africans emotionally as well as intellectually in worship.

In contrast, those African churches that have moved away from some of the styles brought to them by Western missionaries have lively worship that allows them to express themselves holistically. For example, foreigners sometimes mistake prayer meetings for dance parties because dance has become an integral part of African worship. Many African believers look forward to this time of expressing love to God with their whole selves.

How could you creatively foster worship in *your* context?

 **Malaysia:** To help youth make prayer more than simply asking God for things, many Malaysian youth ministries have incorporated concerts of prayer as a regular part of their gatherings of believers. Youth will sometimes spend several hours moving through different elements of prayer. They praise God for who he is through singing, stating names of God and sharing testimonies of his character and work in their lives. They spend time in silent confession—sometimes on their knees and other times with their faces in their hands, expressing shame. Psalms and other Scripture passages are often integrated throughout the concert of prayer. The prayer times include a time of petition and opportunities to pray for rescue from the evil one. While youth initially dreaded the thought of extended prayer times, they now wait with anticipation for the monthly concerts of prayer.

 **Seattle:** Church members have regular opportunities to express themselves during worship in ways other than singing. Newsprint fills the walls of the church and participants write a name or attribute of God for which they are especially thankful. Non-musical members often express their gratefulness for an outlet that extends corporate worship beyond songs.

 **South Africa:** The large gathering of believers in Johannesburg includes a diverse mixture of races at any given service. You better check your pulse if you aren't moved by joining the corporate praise with the multicultural congregation at Rhema Church in Johannesburg. The musical genres pur-

posely reflect the diverse congregation. While a great deal of the country still remains racially divided, Rhema Church and others like it are pictures of the new earth and the body of Christ worshiping together for eternity.

Action Plan for Worship in Your Ministry
- What are strengths and weaknesses of the worship in your ministry?
- How could the priority of worship be strengthened in your ministry?
- What is the first step?

---

3. Community

Priorities

1. Word
2. Worship
3. Community
4. Serving
5. Prioritizing a Few
6. Mobilizing for Outreach
7. Multiplying Leaders

Community is the oneness Christ offers in place of the loneliness produced by sin. As we pursue time with people in their environments and make our ministries a place where love is experienced and expressed, we need to develop community as a regular component of our ministry gatherings for believers.

I recently observed a church in Singapore where the students knew Scripture remarkably well. The people who taught the youth dug deeply into the Word and even allowed for meaningful worship together with the students. In spite of this, everything still felt dead. As I sat back and observed, it became clear that the element lacking in this ministry was community. Youth didn't seem to enjoy being together. Not only did students not talk to one another; it was actually discouraged. They were told that talking with their friends was to be done outside of church. I don't think this accurately reflects what Jesus had in mind for a gathering of believers.

Community is seriously lacking in many ministries. In many churches, turning to greet one another during a worship service is the extent to which people connect with one another. The remainder of the time is often spent passively sitting through the other growth components.

One of my previous ministries had little community when I first started there. Not unlike the church I observed in Singapore, these youth knew the Word of God and attended church regularly, but did not seem engaged. Because it was a large ministry, I was struggling to remember all the youth's names, so I privately asked some of the kids on one side of the room the names of some youth on the other side of the room. They replied, "I don't know." I asked, "Oh, are they new?" They said, "No. They've been here for years. I recognize their faces, but I don't know a thing about them." We didn't eliminate the strong Bible teaching or regular worship, but we worked hard to spend time together so that students would build community. We went bowling together. We went to the beach together. We camped together. I looked for every excuse possible to get together. Youth who had been together for years without knowing each other discovered one another in new ways. Interestingly, the worship, study of the Word and desire to serve became much more alive as well.

Community requires breaking down barriers between people and getting them to work together. It means allowing people to have fun together! Ultimately, spiritual fellowship—deep interaction around kingdom priorities—is the objective of community.

- To what degree is community a part of your gatherings as believers?
- How are you fostering community in your ministry?

Disciplemaking Around the World

Brazil: Birthdays are festive events for Brazilians, so many of our partnering ministries there use birthdays as an excuse to gather Christians together. If you are going to one of these parties, plan on spending most of the day, or at least a full evening of fun, games and plenty of rice and beans. Since sixteenth birthdays are especially important to Brazilians, many youth ministries make them special events. Everyone is asked to bring along a few words to share with the youth having a birthday to affirm God's work in his/her life and challenge him/her to remain faithful.

Australia: St. Martin's Church illustrates a commitment to fostering community among believers. The sanctuary features two open fireplaces to suggest that the church is a "house" of God. Throughout the service, one can smell the soup cooking behind the pulpit in preparation for the communal meal that concludes the weekly gathering of believers. Church members describe their bond as stronger than any other friendships they've known.[5]

 **Chicago:** The other night I met with the guys' cell group that I am leading at my church. To make our study of spiritual gifts more than an exercise in the Word (although a powerful one), we also made it an opportunity to build community. Based on my belief that discovering our spiritual gifts is closely related to the body of Christ affirming those gifts in us, we spent time affirming the gifts that we saw in one another. It was a rich time of building community as well as hearing from God through these inspired words.

How could you foster community in *your* context?

 **New York:** Even large ministries can prioritize community at corporate gatherings of believers. Brooklyn Tabernacle in New York City regularly plans time in their services to break into groups of four or five. For five to ten minutes, people exchange names, share something that is happening in their lives and pray together.

 **Singapore:** All Saints Church in Singapore divides their ministry among cell groups. A great deal of care is given to foster community during the weekly gatherings of cells, but during the in-between times, they use email circles to keep communication flowing. Sometimes the message is just a reminder about the next meeting or a joke to pass along. Other times it's a word of encouragement, a verse or a prayer request. They have found it to further what happens when the group gathers physically.

South Africa: If you want to gather a group of South Africans, include a game of cricket (either playing or watching your favorite team) and some good food to guarantee a good turnout. Many youth ministries make "cricket parties"

a regular part of their programming and look for ways to redeem this gathering. Some of the ministries rent a video to watch after the game that will foster good dialogue among the group about living like Jesus in a fallen world.

Action Plan for Building Community in Your Ministry
- What are the highs and lows of this priority in your ministry?
- What ideas do you have for strengthening this priority?
- What needs to happen first?

---

4. Serving

Serving prioritizes time with others to the extent that we adjust our lifestyles to express care and tangibly meet others' needs. This fourth ministry priority, consistently modeled by Jesus and the early church, is necessary for a complete environment for growth in making disciples.

Serving begins with the ministry leadership. An attitude for serving is contagious—people in our ministries will quickly discern whether we intend to serve or be served.

I have discovered that while people enjoy having fun together and being entertained, there soon comes a point where they will not grow unless we offer more. The most fun I have had with people in ministry has been when we have worked together to help other people, whether painting a widow's house, caring for the children of a single mom, working in a yard, going to a home for elderly people, serving overseas etc. There is nothing like serving together with other believers!

Priorities

1. Word

2. Worship

3. Community

4. Serving

5. Prioritizing a Few

6. Mobilizing for Outreach

7. Multiplying Leaders

- Do you, as a ministry, regularly set aside time to help others in need? If so, assess those times. If not, how can you add this priority?
- Do believers freely meet needs outside the group? If so, how?

Disciplemaking Around the World

Australia: St. Martin's is healthy in this priority as well. This Melbourne congregation has built serving into its core identity. The church building was primarily built by the congregation. A team of women made all the mud bricks. Some of the people who helped were seekers. This value of serving together continues through the people as they grow together.[6]

Cambodia: A thirteen-year-old boy and the youth group he leads go from house to house in Phnum Penn asking people how they can pray for them. Often they find themselves in the ministry of healing people through the power of God, but more importantly, they find themselves with more opportunities to share Christ than they know what to do with.

Hungary: Consuming alcohol has become much more common among Hungarian youth since the revolution. Some of the Christian youth in Budapest regularly visit the pubs to find their peers. They strike up conversations and offer living water that will never leave one thirsty. Though their peers often demean them and reject the invitation to life with Jesus, the Christian youth often stay with them throughout the evening and end up escorting them home in their drunkenness.

How could you encourage serving in *your* context?

India: A pastor at a church in Delhi has a mother who is being denied her old age pension from the tribal government where she lives. She's been told to denounce her faith if she wants to receive it. Since she is unwilling to reject Christ to meet her monetary needs, her son's church cares for her needs by regularly supplying food and other necessary items.

Kentucky: Southland Christian Church in Lexington, Kentucky, with more than six thousand members, serves the community amid the urban sprawl the area is experiencing. Southland is the site for community concerts, plays, elections, aerobics classes, Spanish courses and more. If you need an appliance, furniture or some vegetables, Southland is probably the place to find it. Our ministries should be characterized as places that serve one another.

 **Northern Ireland:** Exodus, a night club in Belfast, is not like most clubs in Europe. It is run by a group of Christians who are targeting youth using hip music and a place to hang out. Christians volunteer their time playing in the band, "bouncing," mingling with people, serving food, etc. As they serve Belfast youth, they see many follow Jesus and join nearby churches.

 **Thailand:** A young girl was thrown out of her tribal home and village because she refused to go to Bangkok to become a prostitute to earn income for her family. Some Christ-followers she met in a neighboring village worked together to make a new home for her. They share their food, clothing, beds and modest homes with her. She now works in a hostel for tribal children, where they learn how to read and write to empower them to earn a living in ways other than prostitution, and she teaches them the Word of God.

Action Plan for Fostering Serving in Your Ministry
- What are the highs and lows of this priority in your ministry?
- What ideas do you have for strengthening this priority?
- What needs to happen first?

Summary

Even if you have been involved in your ministry for a number of years, you may need to devote all your energies to the building phase for a period of time. Remember, this doesn't mean evangelism is non-existent during this phase. Jesus was personally calling people to himself all throughout this period of his ministry as an outgrowth of his love for the Father and for others. However, Jesus didn't emphasize mass evangelism during this first half of his public ministry; he emphasized building a core group of followers.

Though context will significantly shape how believers express love for God and others, believers must universally embrace the Great Commandment through prayer, the Word, Christ, relationships, love and mission. These values are corporately experienced through the Great Commission priorities of Word, worship, community and serving. Churches tend to emphasize one or two of these patterns over the others. All four are needed for a healthy, balanced ministry with believers.

Like the Great Commandment values, these Great Commission priorities should continue to be characteristic of our ministries all throughout their maturing. There is never a point where these are no longer needed.

Notes

[1] Lawrence Richards, *Creative Bible Teaching* (Chicago: Moody, 1998).
[2] George G. Hunter, *The Celtic Way of Evangelism: How Christianity Can Reach the West…Again* (Nashville: Abingdon, 2000).
[3] Ibid.
[4] R. Ellis and C. Seaton, *New Celts* (Eastbourne: Kingsway Publications, 1998).
[5] George G. Hunter.
[6] Ibid.

CHAPTER TWELVE

Equipping Workers to Win Others in Your Context

As observed in chapter seven, Jesus expanded the scope of his ministry by equipping some of his followers to minister alongside him. As he did so, he continued to live out the Great Commandment values of loving God and loving others and called his followers to do the same.

Churches all across the world are filled with hard working believers who are faithfully serving. Many churches claim that twenty percent of the congregation do eighty percent of the work. Sometimes this is simply because leadership has not challenged believers to be involved in the work of the ministry. Other times, it is because workers felt ineffective because they were ministrering without being equipped. Sometimes workers falsely assume that their involvement in ministry means they authoritatively rule those who are not working.

In one of my ministries, I inherited a core group of "leaders." They were elected as a leadership team and when I began to meet with them, I asked them to evaluate the group as a whole in several different areas. We began by assessing the strength of Great Commandment values in the ministry. As each team member gave input, the word consistently used was "they." "*They* never show an interest when we get into the Word. *They* are not very loving toward one another. *They* think prayer is boring," and the accusations continued. Not one of them used a personal pronoun. This group became defensive when I began to turn the questions toward them personally. "Of course we are passionate about these areas," most of them responded. "It's just this group of people we're trying to bring along who are so apathetic!"

Soon after, I made the unpopular decision of disbanding this so-called group of leaders. While initially it appeared like a step backward for the ministry, I knew that for the long-term health of the ministry, we had to follow the process of calling believers to minister who had a heart to serve. We had to challenge people who personally owned the Great Commandment values as a foundation to serving others.

I was reminded of what happened with that initial group of "leaders" a few years later when I was gathered with my new group of workers and asked them to assess our ministry. The first thing one of them said was, "*I* have been so lazy with intentionalize relationships!" Another student talked about the joy he felt as he saw our group exalting Christ together and another commented, "*My* prayer life has been too sporadic and inconsistent." I thanked God for growing a group of workers who now personally embraced the Great Commandment values.

Great Commission Priorities

The Great Commandment values are the true test for those we call to work in the ministry with us.

Equipping workers begins with multiplying the Great Commandment values from our lives into the lives of those who are ready to be equipped. As we do so, we must cast a vision for more workers to share in the work of the ministry and begin training in that regard. A team of workers will surface from that core of believers. We must prioritize time with them and then mobilize them for outreach.

5. Prioritize a Few

Carl Wilson writes:

> The step of ministry training is critical to the expansion of the movement. At this point, most organizations and local churches reach their peak. If they do not train believers other than the pastor to evangelize and build disciples, their expansion stops. The maximum potential is reached without a continuing growth and broadening impact. True multiplication occurs only when disciples are trained in evangelism and disciple-building. No matter how dynamic the pastor, no matter how financially stable and well-organized the church, expansion will not continue if people are not trained to minister.[1]

Priorities

1. Word
2. Worship
3. Community
4. Serving
5. **Prioritizing a Few**
6. Mobilizing for Outreach
7. Multiplying Leaders

Jesus' ability to recruit and equip a few to join him in the work of the ministry required him to intentionalize relationships with them. We see him prioritizing and guarding time with the disciples (Matt. 8:14-15; Mark 1:29-34; 2:13-17; 3:7). As he does so, it becomes clear that Jesus was interested in equipping a team who was available, faithful, teachable and responsive.

Availability: those who make themselves available for ministry (Luke 5:1-3)

Faithfulness: those who are faithful to Christ's expectations for them (Luke 5:4-5)

Teachability: those who are teachable regarding their actions and abilities (Luke 5:6-10a)

Responsiveness: those who are responsive to Christ's leadership (Luke 5:10b-11)

- Who is God calling you to challenge toward something more?
- Which of the above characteristics (availability, faithfulness, teachability, responsiveness) are evident?

How can we help believers move through a process of ministry maturity?   M=Ministry

NON-PEER MINISTRY   **PEER-FOCUSED MINISTRY**

SERVING .... PEER CARE .... PEER EVANGELISM ....…....

DISCIPLEMAKER Task Serving:	People Serving:	Evangelism Projects:	Supportive Relationships:	Redemptive Relationships:	Ministry Community:	Disciple-making Lifestyle:
Task-oriented service projects	Servants to the body of Christ	Sharing our faith on a short-term basis	Ongoing care for peers within the body of Christ	Ongoing care for peers outside of the body of Christ	Influencing peers through planting and reaping with the help of the youth ministry or church	Initiating totally new relationships for the purpose of evangelism and nurture
i.e. Cleaning church, serving food, international construction projects	i.e. Serving with people impact, vacation bible school, nursing home programs, occasional nursery care	i.e. Cross-cultural contacts, sharing our faith outside our normal environment, international ministry projects	i.e. Granting Great Commandment love through the six foundational priorities being applied within our youth group	i.e. Building credible and loving friendships with unbelievers at school, work or home	i.e. Talking with lost friends about God and personally sharing our faith during outreach events	i.e. Strategizing to be a light in an unreached peer arena, whether a sports team, club, or workplace with support of our youth leaders
m^1	$m^1:m^2$	$m^1:m^3$	$m^1:m^4$	$m^3:m^5$	$m^1:m^6$	$m^1:m^7$

As we begin to emphasize the Great Commandment values among the workers God brings our way, we need to equip them both in peer care and peer evangelism. We must equip workers to first focus on caring for others within our group, and then expand to equipping workers to reach their lost peers as well.

- How can we help believers move through a process of ministry maturity?
- How well do your workers express care to the members of the group?

I am amazed at how quickly new believers can lose contact with lost people. Many times, I have had to begin ministry training with workers by simply discussing how to develop relationships with lost people. We need to equip workers with tangible ways to meet and cultivate friendships with lost people.

What lost people would call you their friend? You cannot teach workers to have friendships with lost people if you don't have any lost friends yourself.

Equipping workers for ministry is a process. We must not too quickly send out workers to do outreach without first properly equipping them. As indicated in the diagram below, we may actually have to regulate the momentum by pressing on the brakes ("delay"). Without squelching the enthusiasm of aspiring workers, we must slow them down long enough to equip them.

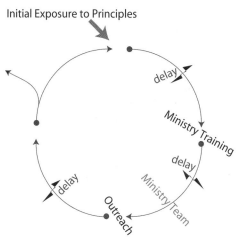

6. Mobilize for Outreach

When should you begin ministry training? When you have people who desire to join you in the work of the ministry and sincerely want to be used by God to make an impact on others. As the Great Commandment values are used to equip a few for the work of the ministry, and as a team of workers join together, the Spirit uses them to win the lost.

As cdhapter 7 discussed, Jesus trained his disciples to use the process of evangelism with people: cultivating, planting and reaping. All too often, modern day ministry has strayed from Jesus' pattern of evangelizing and places all the emphasis upon reaping. This has been a long-term weakness of evangelical churches.

Historically, as the church grew in the Roman Empire, a model of evangelism was developed that used the following process: presenting the Christian message, inviting the individual(s) to accept the message and become a Christian, and if they accept, welcoming them into the church. This is more than reminiscent of the evangelism approaches that characterize many of the churches of which I have been part. The emphasis is upon sharing our message; developing a relationship between the person and the church community is only prioritized after the individual becomes a Christ-follower.

Christianity is more

caught than taught!

In contrast, Saint Patrick developed a movement throughout Ireland that used a process much more reflective of what Christ did. Saint Patrick's process began with establishing relationships with people and bringing them into a community of faith (cultivate). Within that community, they would engage in conversation, ministry, prayer and worship (plant). In time, as the lost discovered that they believed, the Christ-followers invited them to commit (reap). Christianity is more caught than taught! Developing community with lost people enables them to believe and commit.[2]

This is quite different than some of the current evangelistic pursuits in our country that are targeting certain religious groups and seeking to present them with the truth to bring them into the faith. I am sure God can use those approaches of evangelism as well, but they certainly seem to pale in contrast with Jesus' approach, based on a foundation of relationships.

As we make use of the three-fold process of making disciples (cultivate, plant, reap), we must also be aware of the various venues for doing so (one-on-one, small group, large group).

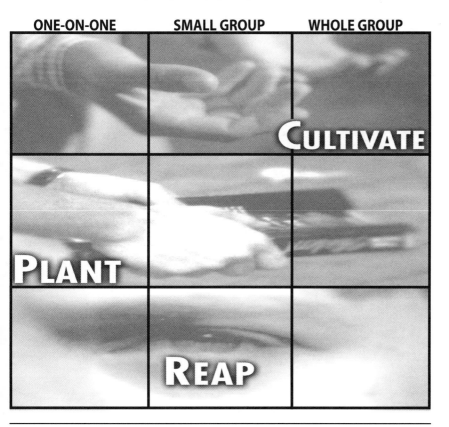

- Which of these nine squares is most natural for you? (i.e. cultivating with a person one-on-one, planting in a large group, reaping in a small group)?
- How can you incorporate all of these venues of evangelism into your ministry?

About two years into one of my youth ministries, we had seen God build our ministry to the point where we were equipping a number of youth to do ministry. We moved slowly into the evangelism phase. We decided we would do one large group outreach together every two to three months. One girl who was passionate about sharing Christ with her friend spoke up in frustration. "I missed the most recent outreach and I have a conflict with this next one we're planning, so this means I can't share Christ with my friend for six months! We have to do these more frequently." Her frustration alerted me that I had not clearly communicated the variety of venues for evangelism. I used this as an opportunity to walk the group through the other ways she could share Christ with her friend. We brainstormed ways she could share Christ one-on-one and with a few friends of hers. We never saw her friend come to Christ during my time there, but her friend heard the gospel many times in many different venues. We must continually equip workers for the privilege and responsibility of evangelism. Evangelism is not solely the job of the ministry leader—it is every believer's calling. A year or so later, we were running large group outreach events almost every week, but we continued to champion and equip youth to use one-on-one and small group venues for evangelism.

For the last several years, many ministries have emphasized event-based evangelism (encouraging people to bring lost friends to a large event where the gospel would be shared) at the expense of equipping people to use small groups and one-on-one venues to share Christ. Now the pendulum is swinging in many ministry contexts against event-based evangelism. Both are necessary. Unless everyone is a fully devoted follower of Christ, equipped and prepared to use their relationships to make disciples, they will need events to prod them along.

- What events does your ministry do in any or all of these 9 categories?
- What do you need to emphasize more?
- Do you sense any adult or young person in your ministry who is desiring something more than just receiving ministry? If so, who?
- Assess their availability, faithfulness, teachability and responsiveness.
- If your group does outreach events, who are the key people involved in the evangelism aspect of the event?
- Is your group ready for the "equipping to win" phase? Why or why not?
- We can evaluate our evangelistic efforts by asking: Are we proclaiming Christ? Do I know how to tell people about Christ? Am I doing it?

- Are our leaders sharing the gospel with lost people?
- Is our group equipped to tell the lost about Christ? Are they doing it?
- Have we prepared our ministry to help believers regularly share Christ with their lost friends?

The end product of evangelism is conversion, the regeneration and renewing of a person by the Holy Spirit.

In our ministries, we can evaluate this area by asking: Are lost people placing their faith in Christ? Included in this evaluation we can calculate our rate and source of growth.

- What percentages of the growth in our ministry are a result of transfer growth (believers from another church), biological growth (babies born into church families) and conversion growth (new followers of Christ)?
- How many people who converted in the lsat year are now part of our fellowship?

There are a number of creative ways to incorporate ministry training and outreach. I just returned from Singapore, where a number of youth gathered for a three-day retreat. During the retreat, they were trained in evangelism with an emphasis on peer care and peer evangelism. As part of the retreat, they each got together with a lost friend for an appointment they had prearranged. Some had coffee, others met at the beach or the arcade. Some spent the time cultivating the friendship, others planting seeds of truth throughout their conversation, and still others challenged their friends to commit to Christ. This event allowed the youth to both be trained and to immediately practice what they learned.

In the Czech Republic, a number of churches gather at English camps throughout the summer. Christians bring lost friends who want to learn English. Prior to the camps, the Christians are trained in evangelism and in how to use the events of the upcoming week to share Christ with their friends. Church groups from English-speaking countries like Australia, Canada, Ireland and the States come for these summer camps to teach English and assist the Czech believers in sharing Christ with their lost friends. As a result, equipped workers fill churches all across Czech and in some neighboring countries. Better yet, there are new believers all across Czech, Poland, Romania and elsewhere who know Christ as a result of this intentional effort for outreach.

We must be reminded that conversion is ultimately a work of God and cannot be controlled by our efforts. However, we are responsible to proclaim the gospel and reach out to the lost. Scripture demonstrates that as we regularly share the gospel, the Lord adds believers to the flock (Acts 2:47; Gal. 6:7). Further, the ultimate goal of evangelism is not the salvation of souls, but the glory of God (John 17:1-5; 2 Cor. 2:14-16; 3:18-4:6).

Summary

Intentionalizing relationships with a few to equip them for the work of the ministry is a non-negotiable. The ministry is to be shared by believers (Eph. 4:11-13). As the leader of the ministry personally and corporately prioritizes the Great Commandment values and as he/she shepherds the flock through the resulting fruit, some of the group will no longer be satisfied with merely receiving ministry.

The primary shepherd must prioritize a few who are available, faithful, teachable and responsive. The few must then be mobilized for outreach by being equipped for peer care and peer evangelism. As they are equipped, they can move people through the process of evangelism (cultivating, planting and reaping) in a variety of venues (one-on-one, small group, whole group).

Notes

[1]Carl Wilson, *With Christ in the School of Disciple Building: A Study of Christ's Method of Building Disciples* (Grand Rapids: Zondervan, 1976), 101.

[2]J. Finney, *Recovering the Past: Celtic and Roman Mission* (London: Darton, Longman and Todd, 1996).

CHAPTER THIRTEEN

Multiplying Shepherds in Your Context

I used to pride myself on turning people away from working with me in ministry if they weren't the best leaders. I would proudly proclaim to people that we only wanted those who were mature in their faith and equipped to serve in this ministry. That brought me a great deal of affirmation from the few who made it in—and an incredible shortage of workers. When I began to look more closely at God's Story, I saw how he consistently allowed people of varying degrees of maturity to be involved in different places in the ministry. I had only wanted people who would pursue relationships with people and who would shepherd them. While those people are absolutely necessary, so are the people who find joy in preparing the food for refreshments, arranging the logistics and setting up for a gathering. Furthermore, the people who shepherd must never become "too good" to serve or they are no longer shepherds with a Great Commandment heart.

One of the most freeing discoveries for me was that just as our ministries have participants at all different phases of spiritual maturity and gifting, so should our team of workers and leaders. Further, not everyone is called to be a leader. Many mature believers are gifted most to serve faithfully as workers, while God has anointed a few to be shepherds of the flock.

From Jesus' large group of disciples, he appointed twelve as apostles. Becoming an apostle did not alleviate the responsibilities they had as workers, it simply added the accountability for other sheep.

> Becoming an apostle did not alleviate the responsibilities they had as workers, it simply added the accountability for other sheep.

In some cultures, leadership is something to which many aspire, while in others it is avoided. We need to identify those God has gifted for leadership from those who have faithfully proven themselves as workers in the ministry. Jesus multiplied himself through proven workers to whom he was ready to give added responsibility. He did not pursue the existing religious leaders; he grew his own. He continued to live out the Great Commandment among his emerging leaders and called them to do the same as they prepared to lead others.

Though multiplication doesn't typically occur until several years into the ministry, the disciplemaking leader must be thinking about multiplication from the beginning. At the same time, multiplying too soon will hinder growth. I have intentionally made this chapter less detailed because most of us need to spend a great deal of time first thinking about building and equipping to win, while seeing the potential for multiplication in the future. Sonlife's advanced training seminars deal more with this phase of ministry.

In my first local church ministry, I tried to drive the disciplemaking process along, and one year in, I claimed we were multiplying leaders. In the long run, we really didn't create a movement of multiplication at all—instead, we had a very weak foundation. I have observed countless other ministries around the world who have made the same mistake as I did. We cannot circumvent the process. At the same time, we need to be mindful of multiplication right from the start of building the ministry, though the restructuring for multiplication should not happen before the ministry is ready. I have included just enough here to plant the seeds for thinking about multiplication but purposely not enough to really minister in a mode of multiplication.

A disciplemaking ministry and its leader(s) must continue to grow in and prioritize the Great Commandment values as God brings the ministry to a point of multiplication. These values, as described earlier, should continue and even deepen.

Great Commission Priorities

7. Multiply Leaders

As Jesus lived out the Great Commandment values among his workers, he identified those to whom he would give greater responsibility, challenged them and appointed them as apostles. We must follow that same process to multiply leaders: identify, challenge and appoint.

1. *Identify* those workers who have been proven and faithful in peer care and peer evangelism and whom God has gifted to shepherd others.

2. *Challenge* those you identify to move toward leading a segment of the ministry, thus expanding the scope of your ministry, internally and/or externally. Challenge them by sharing the vision.

3. *Appoint* those who accept the challenge.

After appointment, equip the apprentice leader to shepherd a segment of the flock through the following process, just as Jesus did.

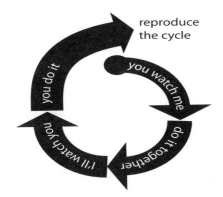

R. N. Longenecker writes,

> Luke makes no catalog of the qualities, characteristics, attitudes, or actions involved in Christian discipleship. What he presents are portrayals of the ministry of Jesus and of the missions of the early Church, particularly the missions of his hero, Paul.[1]

• What are the implications for your ministry? Is there someone you should be challenging to take on a leadership role with you?

Summary

Loving God and loving others will continue to be the foundation of our lives as ministers and of what our ministries consist. We must continually evaluate our personal growth in each of the Great Commandment values, particularly as we look at multiplying ourselves through other leaders.

From those you equip for the work of the ministry, some will be gifted for leadership and allow you to expand the scope of your ministry by multiplying leaders. You must identify whom God has gifted for a position of leadership from those proven as workers. You must challenge, appoint and equip them for a position of leadership in the ministry. The intent is not necessarily for the new shepherd to replace you, but to multiply the amount of influence you and your ministry can have.

As you equip new shepherds, you must model leadership and gradually pass the baton to them. As God moves you through that process together, to the point of releasing them as shepherds on their own, challenge them to start the process over with another group member who is gifted for leadership and proven as a worker.

> I suspect that a lot of people enter the ministry because they don't understand who a shepherd is and what a shepherd does. They think it would be such a neat thing to take up a staff. By gazing at beautiful paintings of barnyard scenes that look so quaint and peaceful, they nurture a romantic view of the pastorate. Yet one thing is true of every barnyard. Barnyards stink. These pictures might come closer to reality if they came in scratch-n-sniff versions.[2]

Notes

[1]R.N. Longenecker, "Taking Up the Cross Daily: Discipleship in Luke-Acts," in *Patterns of Discipleship in the New Testament*, ed. R. N. Longenecker (Grand Rapids: Eerdmans, 1996), 74-75.

[2]E.Glenn Wagner, *Escape from Church, Inc: The Return of the Pastor-Shepherd* (Grand Rapids: Zondervan, 1999),168.

In October 1999, missions leaders from all over the world gathered in Iguassu to assess the past and strategize the future of world missions. The non-Western delegates were asked to assess the Western missions pursuits of the last century. In response, national leaders from all over the world graciously expressed their concern that Western missionaries had presented a monotheistic God to the world. Hearing their input, the Westerners were a bit alarmed, thinking that a monotheistic view of God was a very noble thing to have passed along. The national leaders continued by saying, "You brought us Jesus, but you didn't tell us much about the role of the Father and you especially neglected to tell us about the role of the Holy Spirit."

While I have unashamedly hailed Jesus as the hero of God's Story throughout this look at ministry, I have also sought to regularly point out the need for dependence upon the Father and the role of the Spirit in ultimately bringing about ministry. I would never want one to presume from reading the preceding pages that one can simply focus on certain ministry priorities and expect results. The Holy Spirit must be alive and active in our ministries if we expect to see fruit.

The gospel of Jesus Christ has gone forth in every era with power to change hearts. Today that gospel is the answer to the longings of the postmodern generation. Our task as Christ's disciples is to embody and articulate the never-changing good news of salvation in a manner that every generation in every culture can understand. Only then can we become vehicles of the Holy Spirit in bringing them to experience the same life-changing encounter with the triune God from whom our entire lives derive their meaning.[1]

It is my prayer that engaging anew with the life of Christ might birth or renew in you a passion to connect your journey with the Story of God! I look forward to an eternal deepening of my own understanding of the Story and am awed by God's willingness to let me be part of it. Thank you for the honor of sharing my heart with you. Because of our commitment at Sonlife to lifelong learning, be sure to regularly participate with others in exploring the issues addressed here, both through your own ministry networks and through our web-based, ongoing e-learning at www.sonlife.com.

Notes

[1]Stanley Grenz, *A Primer on Postmodernism* (Grand Rapids: Eerdmans, 1996), 174.

BIBLIOGRAPHY

Allender, Dan. *Intimate Allies*. Wheaton, IL: Tyndale, 1995.

Banks, Robert. *Reenvisioning Theological Education: Exploring a Missional Alternative to Current Models*. Grand Rapids: Eerdmans, 1999.

Buechner, Frank. *Telling the Truth: The Gospel as Tragedy, Comedy, and Fairy Tale*. In *The Sacred Romance: Drawing Closer to the Heart of God*, by Brent Curtis and John Eldridge. Nashville: Thomas Nelson, 1997.

Coleman, Robert. *The Master Plan of Evangelism*. Grand Rapids: Baker Books, 1993.

Crabb, Larry. *The Safest Place on Earth: Where People Connect and are Forever Changed*. Nashville: Word, 1999.

Donaldson, D.L. "Guiding Readers—Making Disciples: Discipleship in Matthew's Narrative Strategy." In *Patterns of Discipleship in the New Testament*, edited by R. Longenecker. Grand Rapids: Eerdmans, 1996.

Ellis, R. and Seaton, C. *New Celts*. Eastbourne: Kingsway Publications, 1998.

Finney, J. *Recovering the Past: Celtic and Roman Mission*. London: Darton, Longman and Todd, 1996.

Freire, Paulo. *Pedagogy of the Oppressed*. New York: Continuum, 1997.

Geertz, Clifford. *An Interpretation of Cultures*. New York: Basic Books, 1973.

Gordon, S.D. *Quiet Talks on Prayer*. New York: Revell, 1904.

Grassi J. *A World to Win: The Missionary Methods of St. Paul the Apostle*. Maryknoll, NY: Orbis, 1965.

Grenz, Stanley J. *A Primer on Postmodernism*. Grand Rapids: Eerdmans, 1996.

Hawthorne, S.C. "Mandate on the Mountain." In *Perspectives on the World Christian Movement*, edited by R. Winter and S. Hawthorne. Pasadena, CA: William Carey Library, 1999.

Hendricks, Howard. *Leadership Journal* (Summer 1980).

Hendricks, Howard. *Leadership Journal* (Summer 1982).

Hodges, Andrew G. *Jesus: An Interview Across Time*. New York: Bantam Books, 1986.

Hofstede, Geert. *Cultures and Organizations: Software of the Mind*. New York: McGraw Hill, 1997.

The Household of God, 20. New York: Friendship Press, 1954.

Hunter, George G. *The Celtic Way of Evangelism: How Christianity Can Reach the West...Again.* Nashville: Abingdon, 2000.

Johnson, Allan. *The Blackwell Dictionary of Sociology: A User's Guide to Sociological Language.* Malden, MA.: Blackwell, 1995.

Konopka, L. "David's Watergate: I'm Pregnant." Blythefield Hills Baptist Church. Rockford, MI, 22 March 1998.

Konopka, L. "Communicating a Vision of Grace" Blythefield Hills Baptist Church. Rockford, MI, 18 October 1998.

Longenecker, R.N. "Taking Up the Cross Daily: Discipleship in Luke-Acts." In *Patterns of Discipleship in the New Testament*, edited by R.N. Longenecker. Grand Rapids: Eerdmans, 1996.

Mayes, Gary and Spader, Dann. *Growing a Healthy Church.* Chicago: Moody Press, 1991.

Ortberg, John. *The Life You've Always Wanted.* Grand Rapids: Zondervan, 1997.

Piper, John. *Let the Nations be Glad: The Supremacy of God in Missions.* Grand Rapids: Baker Books, 1993.

Richards, Lawrence. *Creative Bible Teaching.* Chicago: Moody Press, 1998.

Richards, Lawrence. *A Theology of Church Leadership*. Grand Rapids: Zondervan Publishing, 1980.

Shade, B.J. "The Influence of Perceptual Development on Cognitive Style: Cross-Ethnic Comparisons." In *Early Childhood Development and Care*, 1989.

Sookhdeo, P. "Cultural Issues in Partnership in Mission." In *Kingdom Partnerships for Synergy in Missions*, edited by W. Taylor. Pasadena, CA: William Carey Library, 1994.

Turner, Jonathan H. *A Theory of Social Interaction.* Stanford: Stanford University Press, 1988.

Wagner, E.Glenn. *Escape from Church, Inc: The Return of the Pastor-Shepherd.* Grand Rapids: Zondervan, 1999.

Willard, Dallas. *The Spirit of the Disciplines: Understanding How God Changes Lives.* New York: Harper Collins, 1988.

Wilson, Carl. *With Christ in the School of Disciple Building: A Study of Christ's Method of Building Disciples.* Grand Rapids: Zondervan, 1976.

Wolters, Albert. *Creation Regained: Biblical Basics for a Reformational Worldview*. Grand Rapids: Eerdmans, 1988.

Yancey, Philip. *What's So Amazing About Grace?* Grand Rapids: Zondervan, 1997.